Achieve IELTS

English for International Education

Teacher's Book

Louis Harrison
with
Caroline Cushen
Susan Hutchison

Marshall Cavendish
Education

First published 2005 by Marshall Cavendish Ltd

Marshall Cavendish is a member of the Times Publishing Group

Marshall Cavendish ELT
119 Wardour Street
London W1F 0UW

Editorial, design and production by Hart McLeod, Cambridge

Printed and bound by Edelvives, Zaragoza, Spain

The authors would like to thank Ahmed Hossini, Shirichi Kimura, Hiroko Kobayashi and Jia Han Xu for their hep with the writing section answers.

Contents

Author team

Louis Harrison teaches at the University of Bradford on IELTS preparation courses as well as pre-sessional and foundation courses. He has taught in the UK, Turkey, Hungary, Italy and Sri Lanka and is an experienced author having written several English Language teaching books.

Caroline Cushen is a current IELTS examiner with five years' testing experience overseas and in the UK. She has taught in Spain, Hungary, Indonesia, Malaysia and Vietnam. She is currently teaching on EAP Foundation and MA TESOL Programmes at the University of Buckingham.

Susan Hutchison is a teacher trainer and examiner who worked for many years with the British Council where she was involved in the development of the British Council IELTS CD-Rom project. She has taught in the UK, Italy, Hungary and currently teaches English at The British International School in Moscow.

IELTS and Achieve IELTS

About IELTS

IELTS stands for *International English Language Testing System*. It is one measurement of a student's level of English accepted by colleges and universities in countries such as Australia, New Zealand, the United Kingdom and many others including, increasingly, the United States.

The test has six modules: listening, academic reading, general training reading, speaking, academic writing and general training writing. Candidates choose to do either academic or general training reading and writing, and all candidates do the same listening and speaking test. Candidates who wish to go into higher education do the academic modules, the general modules are for candidates who want to do non-academic training or training for immigration purposes.

The test is scored on a band from 0 (did not attempt the test) to 10 (expert user). The score at which colleges and universities accept students varies from institution to institution, but as a very rough guide, universities may accept students with IELTS scores of 5.5+ for undergraduate degree studies and 6.5 + for postgraduate studies.

The modules are divided into parts and taken in the following order:

- **Listening** – Four sections with 40 questions. Time 30 minutes.
- **Academic reading** – Three passages with 40 questions. Time one hour.
- **General training reading** – Three passages with 40 questions. Time one hour.
- **Academic writing** – Two tasks. Time one hour.
- **General training writing** – Two tasks. Time one hour.
- **Speaking** – Three parts. Time 11 to 14 minutes.

Scoring is provided as an overall score and as individual test scores.

Overall scoring

IELTS results are reported on a nine-band scale. All scores are recorded on the Test Report Form along with details of the candidate's nationality, first language and date of birth. Each overall band score corresponds to a descriptive statement. This in turn gives a summary of the English language ability of a candidate classified at that level. The nine bands and their descriptive statements are as follows:

9 **Expert user** – Has fully operational command of the language. Appropriate, accurate and fluent with complete understanding.

8 **Very good user** – Has fully operational command of the language with only occasional unsystematic inaccuracies and inappropriacies. Misunderstandings may occur in unfamiliar situations. Handles complex detailed argumentation well.

7 **Good user** – Has operational command of the language, though occasional inaccuracies, inappropriacies and misunderstandings in some situations. Generally handles complex language well and understands detailed reasoning.

6 **Competent user** – Has generally effective command of the language despite some inaccuracies, inappropriacies and misunderstandings. Can use and understand fairly complex language, particularly in familiar situations.

5 **Modest user** – Has partial command of the language, coping with overall meaning in most situations, though is likely to make many mistakes. Should be able to handle basic communication in own field.

4 **Limited user** – Basic competence is limited to familiar situations. Has frequent problems in understanding and expression. Is not able to use complex language.

3 **Extremely limited user** – Conveys and understands only general meaning in very familiar situations. Frequent breakdowns in communication occur.

2 **Intermittent user** – No real communication is possible except for the most basic information using isolated words or short formulae in familiar situations and to meet immediate needs. Has great difficulty understanding spoken and written English.

1 **Non user** – Essentially has no ability to use the language beyond possibly a few isolated words.

0 **Did not attempt the test** – No assessable information.

Individual test scores

Listening and Reading

The candidates write their answers on the question paper, but must transfer their answer to an answer sheet at the end of the exam. Candidates may write their answers in upper or lower case letters, and use American or British English. However, candidates should be careful with the spelling and grammar of their answers, and incorrect spelling and grammar are penalised. Where the question asks for no more than two/three words, if the candidate writes more than this the answer is marked as wrong.

Writing

Writing is assessed over nine IELTS bands (which are confidential).

Task 1 is assessed on task achievement, coherence and cohesion, lexical resource and grammatical range and accuracy.

Task 2 is assessed on arguments, ideas and evidence, communicative quality and vocabulary and sentence structure.

If the candidate is under the word length they will lose points, if they have copied they will be severely penalised.

Speaking

Candidates are assessed according to fluency and coherence, lexical resource, grammatical range and accuracy, pronunciation.

About *Achieve IELTS*

Approach to learning and teaching

Achieve IELTS is unique among IELTS courses in that it takes a student-centred approach towards test-preparation. That is, we see the student as the most important part in preparing for IELTS. Furthermore, the course does not see the test as the end-point of the course. From the students' perspective, an IELTS score is simply a way of progressing to their goal: an English-medium education in the subject of their choice in English-medium institutions.

Achieve IELTS provides students with practise for the test and beyond the test by exposing them to typical situations in college and university life, both in academic situations and social situations in an academic environment. An example of an academic situation is attending a seminar; an example of a social situation is meeting other students or sharing accommodation at university.

This approach has many advantages:

1 It reflects the aims of the test itself which 'is designed to test readiness to enter the world of university-level study in the English language and the ability to cope with the demands of that context immediately after entry'. (http://www.ielts.org/teachersandresearchers/faqs/default.aspx#PredictAcademicSuccess)

2 It motivates students by showing life after IELTS – giving them the language necessary to cope with life in another culture and exploring situations and questions they are interested in. Indeed the course can be seen in part as a series of questions asked by students:

- Unit 1 – What happens at registration?
- Unit 2 – How do I find my way around?
- Unit 3 – What happens with accommodation?
- Units 4 and 5 – What is social life like and how can I get involved?
- Unit 6 – What kind of academic work will I do?
- Unit 7 – What are foreign towns and cities like?
- Unit 8 – How can I keep in touch with other people?
- Unit 9 – What facilities are available for sports and recreation?
- Unit 10 – How can I get involved with society outside academic life?

- Unit 11 – Can I work during my studies?
- Unit 12 – How can improve my performance?

3 It provides insights into the culture and traditions of the educational system which the students may be a part of after passing the test.

4 It asks the students to evaluate their own performance, to look at their own strengths and weaknesses in terms of the test – see the Introduction unit.

This approach informs the choice of themes within the units, the structure of each unit and the activities within the units.

Achieve IELTS themes

The topics and themes in the course have been chosen for their interest and relevance to students, according to needs analysis of and feedback from students at the Universities of Bradford and Buckingham. For example, students want to know about social life at college and university, and about accommodation and getting work.

Topics and themes have also been chosen to reflect the test. For example, work on the theme of house sharing includes a passage about work done in the home. This passage includes a detailed logical argument of the kind found in the test.

Common themes, such as accommodation, prepare the students for the test in other important ways in that they may well be asked to talk about where they live in the Speaking test. Familiarity with such themes therefore prepares the students to answer common questions in the Writing and Speaking tests.

Note: the Reading and Writing tests in IELTS, unlike those in *Achieve IELTS*, are not linked thematically. *Achieve IELTS* uses the same theme across all sections for course continuity and to help students to prepare their ideas and opinions about common topics.

Achieve IELTS unit structure

Achieve IELTS Student's Book is divided into three notional parts around which the topics for the units were chosen:

- Units 1–4 deal with social topics such as sharing a house or joining a student society.
- Units 5–8 deal with more technical topics frequently encountered in the test, such as communication technology and sustainable energy.

- Units 9–12 deal with attitudinal topics which ask for students' opinions and attitudes, for example on issues such as social welfare (charities) and work.

Each Student's Book unit is divided into five sections: an introduction to the theme of the unit, then four test practise sections which give the students practise in each of the IELTS sections of reading, listening, speaking and writing.

Introduction

The introductory sections give IELTS practise for part 2 of the listening test, which deals with people in social situations in an academic context. The introductory sections go further, however, by activating the language and expressions from part 2 of the listening test and helping the students to make them part of their own productive language. The introductory sections get the students ready for the rest of the unit and help to prepare them for study in an English-medium university or college.

Test practise sections

The test practise sections are divided into the four components of the IELTS – listening, reading, speaking and writing – although not always in this order.

These sections contain skills development and test practise. Rather than asking the students to do an activity once only (as in the test), a reading or listening passage will usually have at least two activities attached to it in order to

- give the students the opportunity to practise a variety of question types
- give the students deeper understanding of the passage
- exploit the passage in terms of vocabulary and grammar to develop the students' vocabulary and language.

You may, however, wish to exploit any reading or listening passage once only to duplicate test conditions.

The skills practised and the difficulty of the passage have been chosen and graded in terms of the activity style and the language level (see below for language level). Activity styles that are frequently used in the test, such as multiple-choice questions, matching headings with paragraphs, and labelling activities, are introduced and practised from the start of the course.

Activities that demand a lot from the students in terms of language and thought, such as summarising, are practised in the second half of the course when the students feel more confident with their English and with the test.

As *Achieve IELTS* stays as close to the test as possible in terms of instructions, activities and exploitation of passages, you may wish to supplement the questions in the Student's Book with more of your own.

The length and corresponding difficulty of all passages and activities increases throughout the course. Towards the end of the course the students will build up to full-length reading, listening, speaking and writing tasks.

Reading and listening sections are divided into cycles following this pattern:

- **Lead-in** – a short activity, for example a quiz, general questions, vocabulary pre-teaching, using a picture for discussion (usually the large picture at the beginning of a unit).
- **Test practise (1)** – a global comprehension activity, for example matching headings with paragraphs.
- **Test practise (2)** – an activity which asks the students to read or listen to a passage again in greater detail, for example multiple-choice questions.
- **Language study/pronunciation** – where examples of a grammar or pronunciation point occur naturally within the passage, this is brought out, presented and practised.
- **Extension** – a production activity which extends and personalises the theme of the passage or topic, making it relevant and personal to the student.

In sections with more than one passage, this cycle will be repeated.

Listening

Test task types included in the book are monologues and dialogues in social and academic situations, including conversations, seminars, workshops, lectures and talks. Additional listening to social conversations in academic situations is given in all introductory sections.

Reading

The reading sections in the Student's Book cover a wide variety of text types, including articles from magazines and journals, newspaper reports and other sources to reflect the text types in the academic module of IELTS. All have been taken from authentic sources. Practice in the general training module reading test is given in the Workbook.

Writing

Achieve IELTS takes a thorough approach to tasks 1 and 2 of the writing test by providing staged practise of each task. The approach of *Achieve IELTS* to the academic writing tasks is to: break the task into smaller sub-skills; practise these sub-skills; then build back up to the full task. Practise for general training task 1 is in the Workbook.

The writing sections often contain a preliminary reading passage which acts either as a model of how to answer or a warning of how not to answer. This Teacher's Book provides model answers for each writing task, together with samples of students' answers with a comment from an experienced IELTS examiner.

Speaking

The speaking sections build progressively through the three parts of the speaking test: introduction and interview, individual long turn, and two-way discussion. This progression allows the students to focus on each part of the test before putting it all together in full speaking tests at the end of the course. This helps them to understand how the speaking test is staged and what is required at each stage.

In addition to test practise, the course includes fluency activities – fun, engaging, confidence-building activities to improve spoken fluency. These usually precede test practise and if exploited fully can really help the students prepare for the test.

Other features

- **Language study.** The language study sections are intended as revision and practise of major language points which the students have already encountered in previous learning. Examples of these points are taken from listening and reading passages where they occur in context naturally. In order to ensure thorough revision of these language points, practise is given in the Student's Book and further practise is available in the Workbook. It should be noted that while passages and texts have been chosen for their appropriateness to the level and to the language point, the passages will contain language and structures that the students are not taught in the Student's Book, just as the students will come across language and structures they are not familiar with in the test.

- **Pronunciation.** The *Achieve IELTS* pronunciation syllabus focuses on features such as word and sentence stress and intonation. The students are also asked to practise the pronunciation of common colloquial expressions and phrases in the 'Express yourself' sections.

- **Express yourself.** In order to prepare the students for life after IELTS, where appropriate, expressions naturally occurring in listening passages are highlighted for the students' attention. These will be very useful during the time they are at an English-medium university and will also make the students sound more fluent and confident.

- *Achieve IELTS.* During the course the students will be offered instruction on how the test works, advice and suggestions on how to prepare for questions, and examinations strategies to get the best out of the test. We have avoided blanket statements in favour of concrete examination strategies followed up with practice activities that help the students apply the strategy offered. The aim is to present the students with a few real examination strategies and to help them practise and improve.

- **Study skills.** Study skills are presented and practised as part of the Workbook. You may wish to do these sections in the class or give them to the students to do at home. Our experience shows that students with good study skills learn better and more thoroughly that the students who do not practise good study skills. For this reason, the first listening passage in Unit 1 is about good study skills and we strongly recommend that the students follow the study skills syllabus in the Workbook. The study skills syllabus includes:
  - remembering vocabulary
  - keeping a vocabulary notebook
  - revising vocabulary
  - using a dictionary
  - choosing correct meanings from a dictionary
  - dictionary work
  - grouping vocabulary
  - resources in libraries
  - using illustrations and diagrams
  - collocation
  - collocation with *make* and *do*
  - exam preparation.

Achieve IELTS activities

Putting the focus on the students means doing test practise through interaction with other students, not as a single test-candidate facing IELTS alone. For this reason, *Achieve IELTS* includes motivating and stimulating activities involving pair, group and team work. A key principle in our approach is that test practise can be fun (but still hard work). *Achieve IELTS* includes quizzes, pair work and fluency activities to increase motivation and confidence as students prepare for the test. This Teacher's Book offers ideas and suggestions for activities additional to those in the Student's Book.

Achieve IELTS Workbook

Achieve IELTS Workbook contains further practise of:

- all test sections
- pronunciation
- language points.

It also contains practise in the general training modules for

- writing task 1
- reading.

The Workbook contains sections which practise study skills.

Achieve IELTS Teacher's Book

The Teacher's Book contains:

- an introduction to the course and test
- how to use the Student's Book and Workbook
- instructions on activities
- answers to all activities
- model answers to essays
- photocopiable students' answers to essays with comments from an experienced IELTS examiner for classroom use
- additional activities
- background information to academic life and the theme of each unit
- the IELTS scoring scheme
- further references.

Further references

For more information about IELTS, go to the following websites:

- http://www.ielts.org/
- http://www.idp.com/globalexaminationservices/ielts/default.asp
- http://www.ukstudentlife.com/English/Exams/IELTS.htm

For information about student life in Australia and the UK:

- http://www.idp.edu.au/ – student life in Australia
- http://www.britcoun.org/home.htm – the British Council
- http://www.ukcosa.org.uk/ – the council for international education
- http://www.cisuk.org.uk/ – the council for international students
- http://www.prospects.ac.uk – graduate careers website with a section for international students
- http://www.dfes.gov.uk/international-students/ – UK government site for international students

Themes test overview, *Achieve IELTS* Student's Book survey

Vocabulary question and task types *multiple-choice questions, headings, labelling, classification, summarising*

Background reading

This introductory unit gives students an overview of the IELTS, goes over the structure of the test, gives more information about the test, and introduces the task and question types they will practise in both *Achieve IELTS* and in the test. It also familiarises students with the *Achieve IELTS Student's Book* and asks them to think about which questions and task types they need to concentrate on in order to achieve maximum points.

---

1 **Do the quiz.**

Go over the quiz with the students and explain any unknown words, for example *standard* (level of achievement) or *academic* (to do with education, particularly at university or college).

Ask the students to do the quiz and have them compare their answers when they have finished. Alternatively, you may wish to put them in pairs and have them discuss the answers as they work through the quiz.

1.1 **Now listen and check your answers.**

Tell the students they are going to listen to a talk about the test.

Ask the students to listen and check their answers.

Answers

1 A   2 A   3 A   4 B   5 B

1.1 2 **Listen again and complete the chart.**

Go over the table with students.

Explain that they will listen to the passage again and complete the table.

Answers

1 listening, 40 minutes, four parts
2 reading, one hour, three parts
3 writing, one hour, two tasks
4 speaking, up to 14 minutes, three parts

3 **Look through *Achieve IELTS* and answer the questions.**

Go over the questions with the class and ask the students to look through *Achieve IELTS* and answer them.

Answers

1 five – introduction, listening, reading, writing, speaking (not necessarily in this order)
2 in vocabulary boxes in the margin
3 in boxes headed *Achieve IELTS*
4 27 if you count *will* / *going to*, etc. as separate language points

4 **Work in pairs. Discuss the questions.**

Go over the questions with the students, then allow discussion in pairs.

At the end of the discussion, get the answers from one or two pairs.

Open answers

5 **Match the words in A with the definitions.**

Go over the words with the students and explain that they are all types of exam question.

Have the students match the words with the definitions.

Answers

1 classification
2 multiple-choice questions
3 labelling
4 summarising
5 choosing headings

Now work in pairs. Decide which questions or activities are in the listening test and which are in the reading test.

Put the students in pairs and have them decide which questions and activities in A are in the listening test and which are in the reading test.

If you wish, you could have the students look through *Achieve IELTS* to find the answers.

Answers

Listening test: classification, labelling, multiple-choice questions

Reading test: classification, labelling, multiple-choice questions, summarising, choosing headings

6 **Work in pairs. Complete the table with one example of each question type in *Achieve IELTS*.**

Go over the table with the students and ask them to work in pairs and complete it by looking through *Achieve IELTS* and finding examples of each kind of question.

Suggested answers

1 Unit 1, listening, activity 3
2 Unit 10, listening, activity 1
3 Unit 12, listening, activity 3 (note completion); Unit 3, listening activity 8 (sentence completion)
4 Unit 11, listening, activity 3
5 Unit 3, reading activity 3
6 Unit 2, reading, activity 3
7 Unit 7, reading, activity 2
8 Unit 8, reading, activity 6
9 Unit 2, reading, activity 2
10 Unit 9, reading, activity 4
11 Unit 4, reading, activity 3
12 Unit 9, reading, activity 4
13 Units 1–7
14 Units 8–12
15 Unit 1, speaking, activities 1, 2 and 3
16 Unit 4, speaking, activity 2
17 Unit 12, speaking, activity 3

Note: matching activities are also included in *Achieve IELTS* for the listening and reading tests. An example for listening is in Unit 3, listening, activity 2, and an example for reading is Unit 10, reading, activity 2.

Now work in pairs and ask each other the questions.

Go over the questions with the students, then allow discussion in pairs.

At the end of the discussion, get the answers from one or two pairs. You may wish to make a note of the answers to question 2 in order to give the students extra practise in that exam question type during the course.

Open answers

Themes starting university, timetabling, learning styles

Passages an article the first week at university (reading); getting a timetable, good study skills (listening)

Language study present continuous (introduction), present simple (listening)

Express yourself asking for and giving spellings, talking about things in common (introduction)

Achieve IELTS similar and opposite words (reading), referring to titles in reports (writing)

Vocabulary

people and activities *Chancellor, admissions officer, course administrator, fresher, enrol, registration, tuition, lecture, seminar, workshop, tutorial*

places *faculty, department, school, centre, unit, campus*

subjects *medicine, biology, agriculture, computing, engineering, business, art and design, languages, physics, architecture*

charts *bar chart, pie chart, flow chart, line graph, table, row, section, segment, column, horizontal axis, vertical axis, heading, sub-heading*

other *term, degree*

Background reading

The first week in an Australian or British university is called Fresher's Week and the new students are called *freshers*. The week is an extremely busy time for new students who need to register for courses, register at the library and Students' Union, settle into their accommodation, meet new people and get to know their way around their new environment. In addition to this, the majority of students in Britain prefer to live away from home and attend a university in a new city, and so they may need to familiarise themselves with an entirely new area.

Registration day

This section introduces the unit and gives practise in listening test parts 1 and 2 and the speaking test.

1 **Look at the picture above and say what is happening.**

Direct students to the picture and ask the class for one or two ideas of what is happening.

You may like to ask one or two more questions about the picture, for example 'Where are the people? What do you think the white paper is that a lot of the people are holding? Who are the people behind the tables? What happened when you registered for your course and what kind of information did you give to the institution?'.

Answer

Students are registering for their university course.

Now match the words in A with their definitions.

Direct students to box A and go over the words with them.

Ask students to read the definitions and match the words with the definitions.

Answers

1 course administrator
2 enrol
3 admissions officer
4 registration
5 degree

At this point, you may wish to model the words orally for the students and have them practise them.

2 **Read the card and answer the questions.**

Background reading

Registration details are usually sent out to students up to two weeks before registration so that students know their time and place of registration.

Before students do this you may like to explain *Welcome pack* (usually a file containing information about the university, the facilities, the campus, the Students' Union and the course).

Have students read the questions and the text and answer the questions.

Answers

1 1 pm to 2.30 pm
2 in the Small Hall
3 on registration

3 **Read the registration form. Write a question for each section.**

Go over the registration form with students and elicit one or two questions from the class.

Ask students to write at least one question for each section of the form and explain that this will help them to understand the listening passage later. They will also need these questions for activity 5.

Possible answers

1 What is your surname?
2 What is your first name?
3 Which school are you enrolled with?
4 What is the code for your course?
5 What is your telephone number?
6 What is your date of birth?
7 What is your marital status?
8 Do you have an e-mail address? What is it?

 Now listen to a conversation and complete the form for Belen.

Tell students they will listen to a conversation between the Registrar (the person who registers students) and a student.

This activity is an opportunity for students to develop the skill of listening for detail, and to practise part 2 of the listening test.

Play the listening passage. Students should listen and complete the registration form.

Answers

1 Pérez
2 Belen
3 of Management
4 N100 Bsc-BMS
5 55046
6 3/12/86
7 single
8 bperez@bradford.ac.uk

 4 **Listen again and answer the questions.**

You may like to inform students that in the IELTS they will only hear a listening passage once, but that in order to develop their listening skills they will listen again for comprehension.

Go over the questions with the students and explain *marital status* (whether the person is married or single).

Play the CD and have students listen and answer the questions.

Answers

1 They do not want the wrong name on her student card.
2 It is not connected yet.
3 She has to have her photo taken for her student card.

Express yourself: asking for and giving spellings

Students will encounter these phrases in a number of situations:

- in the listening test (saying and spelling names is a regular feature)
- in the classroom (they may need to spell their name for another student)
- if they go to an English-medium university or college.

Note: spelling names is not part of the speaking test.

Go over the phrases and check that the students understand them

Note that it is becoming common, especially over the telephone, to clarify spellings by referring to the first letter of a word, hence *R for river*. It could be any word beginning with R, however common ones are *Romeo* and *Rodger*.

Now listen and practise.

Play the recording and have students listen and practise, paying attention to pronunciation and intonation.

5 **Work in pairs. Ask each other questions and complete the registration form.**

Refer students back to the questions they wrote for activity 3 and the registration form.

Put students in pairs and have them ask each other questions to complete the form. You may want to supply the students with a course code for question 4.

Open answers

➤ **Further practice:** *Achieve IELTS Workbook,* Unit 1 Vocabulary

6 **Work in pairs. Decide what you can talk about when you first meet another student.**

Go over 1–5 with the students, then put students in pairs and ask them to discuss which things they think students in Australia and the UK feel comfortable talking about at a first meeting.

Answers

1 ✓ 2 ✓ 3 ✓ 5 (if they know the name of their tutor) ✓

Go over the answers and remind the students that we usually avoid talking about money (option 4) until we know a person quite well.

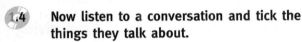

Now listen to a conversation and tick the things they talk about.

Play the recording and have the students tick the things the students talk about.

Answers

✓ 1 ✓ 2 ✓ 3

7 **Label the diagram. Use the words in B.**

Go over the words in B and make sure students understand them.

Ask the students to label the diagram.

Answer

1 faculty 2 school 3 department 4 centre/unit

Background reading

Universities are organised in many different ways according to the individual institution. Generally, a university will be divided into faculties, then schools, then departments and finally centres or units. Faculties and schools are the highest division and these terms are often used interchangeably.

Now listen again and answer the questions.

Go over the questions with the students and play the recording.

Answers

1 Marketing
2 Tao: Business and Marketing Studies, Belen: International Business and Management

3 He is trying to decide whether to do the three-year course or the four-year course.
4 They want to talk about their accommodation and whether they should stay for three years or four years.

Language study: present continuous

8 **Study the examples and explanations.**

Go over the examples and explanations with the students. Explain that the present continuous is often used in connection with a course as there is quite a long period of time in which students are in the middle of the action (the course). As the present continuous has the sense of a present action or event in progress, we often use it to talk about things in the near future and also for making plans and arrangements. Note that the continuous form of a verb cannot be used with verbs that describe a state, or stative verbs such as *like, want, please, surprise, believe, know, understand, hear, see, love.*

If you wish, you could play the recording again for the students to listen for the examples in context of the present continuous.

Now complete the conversation. Use the words in C.

Go over the conversation with the students and have them complete it.

Go over the answers with the class.

You may like to model the conversation orally for the class and have the students practise it in pairs.

Answers

1 A: Hi Vicky, what are you doing?
2 B: I am going to the Small Hall to register.
3 A: What course are you taking?
4 B: I am doing Economics and Development Studies.
5 A: Are you taking the three- or four year course?
6 B: Don't ask! I am still trying to decide.

Express yourself: talking about things in common

One thing we try to do when we meet someone for the first time is to find out things we have in common.

Remind the students of the conversation in activity 7 and go over the phrases.

1.5 **Now listen and underline the stressed words.**

Play the recording and have the students underline the stressed words.

If you wish, play the recording again and have the students listen and practise the phrases.

Answers

We're <u>both</u> in the <u>same</u> <u>hall</u>.

We're <u>probably</u> taking <u>similar</u> <u>subjects</u>.

I'm <u>also</u> taking an <u>undergraduate</u> <u>degree</u>.

We've <u>certainly</u> got <u>something</u> in <u>common</u>.

Aren't <u>you</u> in the <u>same</u> <u>hall</u> as <u>me</u>?

<u>Yes</u>, <u>me</u> <u>too</u>.

9 **Go around the class and find a student you have three things in common with.**

Give the students a few minutes to prepare questions for each other.

If you wish, you could give the students one or two examples: 'Where are you staying? What subject do you want to study?'

Have the students stand up, introduce themselves to another student, and try to find out three things they have in common.

Give them a two-minute time limit per student.

At the end of the activity, ask the students to tell you who they have most in common with.

Open answers

Speaking

Go over the IELTS tasks with the students and make sure they understand what they will practise in this section.

1 **Match the words and phrases with the pictures.**

Direct the students to the pictures and ask one or two students to describe them.

Ask the students to identify the differences between the situations, and also what other greetings they could use, for example, for picture A *I'd like to introduce myself, could I introduce myself*; for picture B *hi, hello*; for picture C *good afternoon, good evening*.

Answers

1 B   2 C   3 A

2 **Work in pairs. Tick the topics the examiner may ask you about.**

Go over 1–6 and tell students they should think about the first few minutes of the speaking test when the examiner will ask a few introductory questions to put them at ease and try to make them feel less nervous.

Point out that, again, we usually avoid talking about things we consider personal at a first meeting, for example appearance, money, family and so on.

Answers

1 ✓   2 ✓   3 ✓   5 (possible, but unlikely)
6 ✓

Now match topics 1–6 with questions A–E.

Go over the questions with the students and ask them to match the questions with the topics. Note that as they will not be asked about one of the topics, there are only five questions (there is no question for 4 as it will not arise in an interview).

Answers

A (What do you do?) 2 (your job)

B (What subject(s) are you taking?) 3 (your studies)

C (Do you come from a large family?) 5 (your family)

D (Are you from this area?) 1 (your hometown)

E (How long did it take to get here?) 6 (your journey)

3 **Decide who says these sentences. Write *examiner* or *candidate*.**

Go over one or two sentences and explain that the students should decide who says the sentences in the context of this scenario and that the sentences are not in the correct order.

Have the students decide whether the examiner or candidate says each sentence.

Answers

Not too far, about half an hour away. – candidate

How are you today? – examiner

Could you spell that for me, please? – examiner

My name is Erzsébet. – candidate

It's E-R-Z-S-É-B-E-T, but you can call me Liz – it's easier. – candidate

Yes, of course it's 062 226. – candidate

And your name is....? – examiner

Not so good. The traffic is terrible in the city centre. – candidate

How was your journey here? – examiner

Very well thank you. – candidate

Do you live far away? – examiner

Can you tell me your candidate number? – examiner

Now order the conversation.

Get the answers from the class and have them put the conversation in order. You may like to ask students to work in pairs to do this.

Answers

How are you today?

Very well thank you.

And your name is ...?

My name is Erzsébet.

Could you spell that for me, please?

It's E-R-Z-S-É-B-E-T, but you can call me Liz – it's easier.

Can you tell me your candidate number?

Yes, of course it's 062 266.

How was your journey here?

Not so good. The traffic is terrible in the city centre.

Do you live far away?

Not too far, about half an hour away.

1.6 4 **Listen and check your answers.**

Play the recording and have the students check their answers.

The students will practise the conversation after some pronunciation work.

Pronunciation

1.7 5 **Listen and write the numbers, dates and addresses.**

Tell students that they will listen to two numbers, two dates and two addresses.

Play the recording once and have the students write the figures. If necessary, play the recording again pausing after each figure.

Answers

1 011388

2 13th September 1985

3 117 Horton Road

4 Wednesday 16th December

5 5.5

6 12 Richmond Road

1.8 6 **Listen and practise the addresses and numbers.**

Play the recording again and have students listen and practise the numbers, dates and addresses.

....

Additional activity: dictation bingo

Write 12 more numbers, dates and addresses on the board.

Have students draw a six-square grid and copy a figure into each of the squares so they have a grid with six random figures.

Explain to the students that you will say the figures to them and when they hear a figure they have written they should cross it out until all the squares are crossed. The first student to cross out all the figures is the winner.

Say the figures on the board at random until a student says they have finished.

....

▶ **Further practice:** *Achieve IELTS Workbook*, Unit 1 Pronunciation

7 **Work in pairs. Practise the conversation in 3.**

This activity simulates a possible conversation in the IELTS and familiarises students with the test. Refer the students back to activity 3.

If you wish, play the recording again.

Have students practise the conversation.

If you wish, ask students to change the conversation to make it personal to them and practise again.

Reading

Go over the IELTS tasks with the students and make sure they understand what they will practise in this section.

1 **Match the words in D with the definitions.**

Go over the words in D with the students and have them match the words with the definitions. Explain that the words are all connected with university life.

Answers

1 tuition

2 fresher

3 lecture

4 term

5 campus

6 Chancellor

2 This reading passage has five sections A–E. Choose the most suitable heading for each section from the list.

Go over the list of headings.

Explain that the passage is about the first week at university and ask the student what they think happens and why the title says a guaranteed good time.

If you wish, write the students' answers on the board and, after checking the answers, see if their guesses were correct.

Answers

1 A = vi   2 B = vii   3 C = i   4 D = iii   5 iv

Background reading

A problem sheet contains a task or problem for students to study or work through before they go to a tutorial or seminar.

---

3 Read the passage again and choose four letters a–g.

Go over a–g with the students.

Have the students read the passage again and choose four of the endings to complete the sentence.

Answers

a Yes – 'settle into their accommodation' (line 5).

b Yes – 'The Students' Union is where students spend most of their of evening in fresher's week' (line 17).

c Yes – 'to receive an introductory talk from the Chancellor' (line 6).

d No. Fresher's week is the wrong time to do this.

e No.

f No. Students do this when the course begins.

g Yes – 'given your passport to student life – the Students' Union card' (lines 14–15).

Achieve IELTS: words with similar and contrasting meanings

Often in reading and listening passages, the answer is contained in a word or phrase with a similar or sometimes contrasting meaning to the word in the question. Identifying key words and phrases in the question and their synonyms and antonyms is a key skill in IELTS and needs to be practiced at every opportunity.

Now find two more examples of a similar word and phrase and a contrasting word or phrase in the reading passage and a–g in 3.

Answers

move into – settle into (line 5)

read – go over (line 24)

are in (the Students' Union) – spend (time) (line 17)

first name – surname (line 12)

receive – are given (line 14)

4 Work in pairs. Decide which things are the same in your country.

Go over 1–5 with the students.

Put students in pairs and have them discuss 1–5. At the end of the activity, get one or two answers from the students.

If you wish, you could put students in groups for the next activity.

Open answers

Now discuss the main differences between ...

Go over 1 and 2 and have the students discuss the topics.

At the end of the activity, get one or two answers from the students.

Open answers

➤ **Further practice:** *Achieve IELTS Workbook,* Unit 1 Reading

Listening

Go over the IELTS tasks with the students and make sure they understand what they will learn in the section.

There are two listening passages: the first is about getting a timetable, the second is about good study skills.

1 Work in pairs. Discuss the questions.

Go over the questions with the class and have the students discuss them in pairs.

At the end of the activity, get one or two answers from the students.

Open answers

2 Match the words in E with the definitions.

Go over the words in E with the students and explain that they are different kinds of class at university.

Ask the students to match the words with the definitions.

Answers

1 workshop
2 seminar
3 tutorial

3 Listen to a conversation between a student and course administrator. Circle T (true) or F (false).

Direct the students to the picture and ask them to describe it.

Explain that the activity will give them practise for part 2 of the listening test.

Play the passage and have the students listen and circle true or false.

Answers

1 True
2 False (only Wednesday afternoon is free)
3 False (there are two: French and Japanese)

Now listen again and complete the timetable.

Go over the timetable and ask the students one or two questions about it, for example 'When is Foundations of Marketing? Where are Languages for Business?'

For weaker students, you may wish to write the answers on the board before they listen to make it easier to complete the timetable.

Play the passage again and have the students complete the timetable.

Answers

1 main lecture theatre
2 2–3
3 seminar
4 Information
5 workshop
6 2–3
7 Global Economics
8 tutorial
9 Environmental
10 Japanese

Language study: present simple

4 Study the examples and explanations.

Go over the examples and explanations with the students.

If you wish, play the passage again so that students can listen to the examples again.

Explain that we use the present simple to talk about states that exist over long periods. This includes general truths (*water freezes at 0ºC*), permanent states (*I'm from Canberra, I'm Australian*) and timetables (*the 9.45 flight from New York lands at 5.30*).

Now work in pairs. Student A, turn to assignment 1.1. Student B, turn to assignment 1.2; ask Student A questions to complete your timetable.

Explain that Student A is the course administrator and has all the timetable details and that Student B needs to ask questions to complete their timetable.

Put the students in pairs.

Have Student A turn to assignment 1.1 and Student B turn to assignment 1.2. The pairs then complete the task.

Go over the answers with the class.

Answers

1 10–11
2 Seminar room 2
3 Languages for Business – Chinese
4 1–3
5 Study skills
6 Main lecture hall
7 Foundations of Production
8 General tutorial

➤ **Further practice:** *Achieve IELTS Workbook,* Unit 1 Language study

5 Do the quiz.

Go over the quiz with the students and teach any unknown words, such as *frustration.*

If you wish, put the students in pairs to compare their answers.

Now turn to assignment 1.3 and read your results.

Have the students turn to assignment 1.3 and read the result of the quiz.

Get one or two answers from the students.

6 Work in pairs. Discuss your results.

Put the students in pairs and have them discuss their results.

Ask the students if they find their results interesting and if they agreed with it.

1.10 7 Listen to a seminar and circle A–C.

Tell the students they will listen to a seminar.

Explain that the activity will give them practise for part 3 of the listening test.

Go over the questions with the students.

Play the passage and have the students circle the answers.

Go over the answers with the class.

Answers

1 B   2 B   3 B   4 C   5 A

1.10 Now listen again. Complete the notes with no more than three words for each answer.

Go over the notes with the class and explain any new vocabulary.

Play the passage again and have the students make notes. Make sure that they only use three words or less for each answer.

Play the passage once more, if necessary.

Answers

1 a good learner
2 at university
3 three-module course
4 organise information
5 ideas and information
6 examples
7 an active part
8 asking questions
9 of the subject
10 an advantage
11 reading list
12 department's website
13 come up with
14 test
15 your tutor

Now work in pairs. List three more good study habits.

Put the students in pairs and have them think of more good study habits.

Get one or two answers from the class and write them on the board.

Additional activity: good study habits

Additional activity: good study habits

Once you have collected the answers, you could ask students to choose one of the activities and ask the whole class whether they do this.

When the students have finished, put the results on the board and find the most popular good study habit.

Writing

Go over the IELTS tasks with the students and make sure they understand what they will learn in the section.

Background reading

Traditionally, subjects have been divided into either arts or sciences. In the early half of the twentieth century, with the emergence of social sciences like sociology, this division became harder to maintain. Nowadays, there are many multi-discipline and cross-discipline subjects, but the basic division here holds more or less true for many subjects.

1 Work in pairs. Put the subjects in F into groups.

Go over the subjects in box F with the class and make sure they understand them.

Put the students into pairs and have them divide the subjects into groups.

Suggested answers

1 arts: art and design, languages
2 sciences: medicine, biology, physics, engineering, computing
3 social sciences: agriculture, business, architecture

▶ **Further practice:** *Achieve IELTS Workbook*, Unit 1 Vocabulary activities 2, 3 and 4

2 Label 1–5. Use the words in G.

Go over the words in box G with the students and direct them to the pictures.

Explain that they will need to know the names and parts of charts, tables and diagrams for the writing test.

Ask the students to label 1–5 with the words.

Answers

1 bar chart   2 pie chart   3 flowchart
4 line graph   5 table

Now label 6–12. Use the words in H.

Go over the words in box H with the students and ask them to label 6–12.

Answers

6 vertical axis   7 horizontal axis   8 section/segment   9 heading   10 sub-heading   11 row   12 column

3 **Look at the charts on the following page and answer the questions.**

Direct the students to the charts and go over the questions.

Have the students answer the questions.

Answers

1 students in UK higher education by number and by subject
2 approximately 230,000 (130,000 in computer science, 50,000 in medicine and dentistry, 50,000 in engineering and technology)
3 27%
4 the number of students over time, or trend
5 open answers

4 **Look at the charts in 3 again and complete the sentences.**

Direct the students to the charts and ask them to complete the sentences.

Answers

1 pie chart, percentage, section (or segment), Business and administrative
2 line graph, vertical axis, horizontal axis, time

Achieve IELTS: referring to titles

During the writing test, students should try to avoid copying the information in the question's title word for word as this will loose marks. It is much better to pick out the key words and write a paraphrase around these.

5 **Read the title and underline the key words.**

Ask the students to read the title and underline the key words.

If you wish, ask one or two students to give you their answers and write them on the board. See if the students can then rephrase the title in their own words.

Possible answer

The chart below shows the <u>number of students</u> in <u>Australia</u> by <u>subject</u> in <u>2003</u> and <u>2002</u>. Write a <u>report</u> for a university lecturer <u>describing the information</u> shown below.

Now write the introduction to your report.

Ask the students to write a short paragraph introducing the report. At this stage, this level of work is sufficient. From Unit 5, the students will be required to write full reports. However, if you wish, you may also ask the students to write the rest of the report.

Suggested answer

The bar chart shows how many students took which subjects between 2002 and 2003 in higher education in Australia. The vertical axis shows the number of students in thousands. The horizontal axis shows the students by year and ten academic subjects which students took.

> **Additional activity: your country**
>
> If you wish, you could try to find similar statistics for your country (often available from a central office for statistics) and give these to the students along with a similar title for additional practise.

➤ **Further practice:** *Achieve IELTS Workbook*, Unit 1 Writing; Unit 1 Study skills

Themes places at universities, directions, types of university, changes in higher education

Passages types of university in the UK (reading); a campus tour, virtual universities (listening)

Language study giving directions (introduction), general amounts (reading)

Express yourself asking for repetition (introduction)

Achieve IELTS repeated information (listening)

Vocabulary

places at university *radio station, student information centre, auditoriums, art gallery, nightclub, cinema, student computing, bursar's office, admissions office, international office, refectory, Students' Union, lecture halls*

subjects *maths and statistics, sociology, humanities*

Information technology *wireless network, modem, workstation, webcam, video conferencing, server, cluster room*

changes *increase, decrease, rise, drop, fall, reduction, decline, levelling off*

other *financial aid*

Background reading

Universities can be divided into a number of categories: by their funding (public or private), by their location (city or campus), by their purpose (technical, e.g. the Massachusetts Institute of Technology, or general), or by their age. Perhaps the most common way of classifying universities is whether the university buildings are together on one site or *campus*, or whether they are integrated into the city, as at the University of London or the University of New York. In Britain, universities can be established in two ways: by Royal Charter from the King or Queen, or by a government act. Many former polytechnics in Britain became universities by government act. Unit 2 also looks at two additional university types: the Open University, an existing UK university where students learn through television and radio broadcasts together with short courses generally during summer; and the Virtual Campus, a university of the future where students will be able to take courses delivered entirely via information technology.

Getting around

This section introduces the unit and gives practise in listening test parts 1 and 2 and the speaking test.

1 Look at the pictures and answer the questions.

Ask the students for the meaning of *campus* and explain it to them if necessary.

Direct the students to pictures A and B, go over the questions and ask them how they know which university is city-based and which is campus-based.

Get the answers from the class. You may wish to ask the students which universities in their country are campus or city universities, and have a short discussion about which are better and why.

Answers

1 Picture A is a city university (University of London), Picture B is a campus university (University of Bradford).

2 The main difference is that a campus university has most of its buildings in one area. By contrast, with a city university the buildings are not in the same location. Other differences are that campus universities are often built outside a city, that students live on campus, and that all the facilities, including entertainment facilities, are on campus.

Note: while the University of London can be considered as a city university, it has many campuses, some of them outside the city.

2 Match the places with the definitions.

Go over the places and definitions with the students and then ask them to complete the matching exercise.

Answers

1 a   2 d   3 f   4 b   5 c   6 e

> **Background reading**
> Other important places at university include the Chaplaincy (the office of the university chaplain or priest), the careers advice service, learning support services (often including the library), and IT support services (computing support).

1.11 Now listen to three conversations and label map A. Start from the Richmond building.

Direct the students to map A and explain that they will listen to three short conversations.

Tell the students that map A is a map of the university in picture B – the University of Bradford.

Ask the students to find the Richmond building, the Communal building and the Phoenix building on the map.

Play the passage and have the students label the map.

Answers

1 the Students' Union   2 art gallery
3 the refectory

1.12 3 Listen to a conversation and circle A–C.

Go over the multiple-choice questions with the students and explain any unknown words, for example *pharmacology* (the study of medicine or pharmacy).

Play the passage and have the students circle the correct letter.

You may wish to play the passage again for the students to check their answers.

Answers

1 B   2 A   3 B

Express yourself: asking for repetition

When they do not understand something, the students should be encouraged to ask the person to repeat their sentence again. Explain that if they do not understand something in the test, it is better to ask the examiner to

repeat him/herself, using one of these phrases, than not to say anything. The student will not lose points for this, in fact it shows they have enough confidence and language to ask the examiner to repeat themselves.

Go over the sentences with the students and ask them to underline the words they think are stressed.

Answers

<u>Sorry</u>, could you <u>repeat</u> that <u>last sentence</u>?
<u>Sorry</u>, I didn't quite <u>catch</u> that.
Can you <u>say</u> that <u>again</u>?
Did you say go <u>left</u> across the <u>park</u>?

1.13 Now listen again and practise.

Play the recording for the students to check their answers and to practise the sentences with the correct sentence stress.

Language study: giving directions

4 Study the examples and explanation.

Go over the examples and explanation with the students.

Explain that when giving directions we don't often use points of the compass, such as north, south and so on. Instead, we use landmarks like a public building, library, church or pub (a pub is especially common in UK directions), or a feature like a statue or a park.

Explain that directions are often given with the base verb and preposition.

Now complete the sentences. Use the words in A.

Direct the students to map A again. Explain that they are starting from the Phoenix building and the directions are to the art gallery.

Answers

1 across   2 towards   3 to   4 between   5 past
6 forward

5 Compete the conversation. Use the words and phrases in B.

Direct the students to map B and explain that it is a map of the university in picture B – the University of London.

Tell the students that the directions are from the Union building to the Brunei Gallery and have them complete the directions with the phrases in B.

Answers

1 tell me the way   2 head for   3 get to
4 go straight ahead

➤ **Further practice:** *Achieve IELTS Workbook,*
Unit 2 Language study

Pronunciation

 1.14 6 Listen and notice how the voice rises and falls.

Play the recording and have the students listen to the phrases and notice the intonation in the phrases. If you wish, you may want the students to write them down.

Now listen again and practise.

Play the recording again and ask the students to practise the phrases.

7 Work in pairs. Use map B and have a similar conversation.

Put the students in pairs and ask them to write a similar conversation using map B.

Have the students practise their conversation.

If you wish, you could ask one or two pairs to act out their conversation for the class.

> **Additional activity**
>
> If you wish, you could extend asking for and giving directions beyond the campus by bringing in maps of your town or city and using these for further pair work practise.

Reading

Go over the IELTS tasks with the students and make sure they understand what they will practise in this section.

1 Work in pairs. Answer the questions.

Go over the questions with the students.

Put the students in pairs and ask them to discuss the questions.

Get the answers from the class at the end of the discussion.

Open answers

2 The reading passage has six sections A–F. Choose the most suitable headings for sections A–F from the list of headings.

Go over the title of the reading passage and the list of headings with the students. Explain any unknown words, for example *polytechnics* (higher educational institutions designed to prepare people for technical and practical work).

Ask the students what they think the passage will contain.

Ask the students to read the passage quickly and match the headings with the paragraphs.

Answers

1 A = ii   2 B = iii   3 C = vi   4 D = vii
5 E = iv   6 F = i

3 Answer the questions using no more than three words from the passage for each question.

Go over the questions with the students.

Ask the students to read the passage again and answer the questions in no more than three words.

Answers

1 the industrial revolution
2 expand higher education
3 vocational and professional
4 social life/academic life

4 Classify the following descriptions as referring to ...

Go over the descriptions with the students.

If you wish, have the students classify the descriptions from memory. Otherwise, refer them back to the passage and have them classify the descriptions.

Answers

1 NU (lines 22–23)
2 UC (line 33)
3 OU (line 36–37)
4 OU (lines 4–5)
5 CU (lines 12–13)
6 FP (line 29)

5 Work in pairs. Discuss the questions.

Put the students in pairs.

Ask them to discuss the questions.

At the end of the discussion, get one or two answers from the class.

Open answers

Language study: general amounts

6 Study the examples and explanation.

Go over the examples and explanation with the students.

Explain that we do not need to give specific amounts with groups or classes of things. Referring to a general amount is usually enough in these cases.

Then have the students order the phrases in C.

Possible answer

most of, many of, several, a number of, some, not many

7 Read the passage in 2 again, and underline words and phrases for general amounts.

Refer the students back to the passage again, specifically paragraphs D–F, and have them underline the phrases for giving general amounts.

Possible answers

paragraph D for many years, many became universities

paragraph E are made of several smaller colleges

paragraph F some city campuses

Now complete the passage. Use the phrases in C.

Have the students complete the passage with the words in box C.

Answers

1 most of   2 many of   3 most
4 not many of   5 most

8 Write the questions in full.

Go over the questions. If you wish, do the first one with the class as an example.

Ask the students to write the questions in full.

Check the answers with the class.

Answers

1 Would you like to study abroad?
2 Which country would you like to go to?
3 What kind of university would you like to go to: city or campus university?

Now add two more questions.

Ask the students to write two more of their own questions.

Open answers

9 Ask five students the questions and note their answers.

Have the students ask at least five more students the questions. They must take a note of the students' answers as they will need them for the next activity.

Now write about your findings.

Ask the students to write about the findings to their questions.

Make sure they use some words and phrases for general amounts.

➤ **Further practice:** *Achieve IELTS Workbook,* Unit 2 Reading

Speaking

Go over the IELTS tasks with the students and make sure they understand what they will practise in this section.

1 Work in pairs. Tick the phrases that are suitable to introduce a topic and put a cross next to the phrases that are not suitable.

Go over the phrases with the students and explain that most of the phrases can be used to introduce a topic.

Put the students in pairs and ask them to decide which topics should not be used to introduce a topic.

Answers

The students should not use:

Listen up … (very informal)

I'd like to introduce the topic of a place I have studied … (there is no need to include the title of the topic, this is repetition)

2 Read the topic and tick the subjects in D that you could talk about.

Explain to the students that they will practise part 2 of the speaking test.

Go over the topic with the students and refer them to the sub-topics in D. Explain that in the test they will have one minute to make notes on the topic.

Work through an example with the students. For example, for *number of students in class* they could include the ages of their classmates, gender, subjects their classmates studied, nationality and so on.

Have the students decide which subjects they could speak about.

Answers

All subjects are acceptable except *crime* and *food*.

Now make notes on three of the subjects in D.

Ask the students to choose three of the subjects and make notes about them.

Tell the students they will use the notes in activity 6.

3 Order the questions.

Explain to the students that they should order the words to make questions, and should make sure they get the word order and punctuation correct.

Answers

1 Can you tell me about a place you really enjoyed studying at?
2 Why did you go there?
3 How many students studied with you?

1.15 Now listen to an interview and check your answers.

Explain to the students that they will hear an extract from an IELTS interview and they should listen and check their answers.

Play the recording for the students to check their answers.

1.15 4 Listen again and note any more rounding-off questions.

Explain to the students that after part 2 of the test – the individual long turn – the examiner may ask one or two follow-up questions to lead into the topic.

Play the recording again and have the students make a note of the other follow-up questions, pausing after each question, if necessary.

Answers

When was the university founded?
Why did you go there?

5 Choose a topic and write two or three rounding-off questions.

Go over the topics and ask the students to write two or three rounding-off questions.

Get one or two answers from the students.

Open answers

6 Work in pairs. Student A, use your notes and talk about the topic in 2 for two minutes. Student B, ask Student A the rounding-off

questions in activities 3 and 4. Begin *Can you tell me about ...*

Explain to the students that they will practise part 2 of the speaking test.

Student A will talk about the topic using their notes from activity 2. Student B should use the rounding-off questions they wrote down in activities 3 and 4.

Ask them to begin with *Can you tell me about + topic.*

Now change roles.

When the students have finished, ask them to swap roles and do the role play again.

Additional activity: recording

If you wish, you could record the students as they practise for part 2 of the speaking test. Keep the recording until the end of the course and play it back for the students to check their progress.

Listening

Go over the IELTS tasks with the students and make sure they understand what they will practise in the section.

There are two listening passages: the first is a campus tour, the second is a seminar about virtual universities.

1 Work in pairs. Decide which facilities in E are at the University Centre and which are at the Students' Union.

Explain to the students that they will listen to part of a campus tour around the University of Victoria, Canada.

Go over the places in E and make sure the students understand any unknown words, for example *auditorium* (a large room for giving talks and lectures).

Put the students in pairs.

Go over the first place as an example. Ask the students if they think the radio station is part of the University Centre or the Students' Union.

Put the students in pairs and ask them to decide which facilities belong to the Students' Union or the University Centre.

Then play the passage and have the students listen and check their answers.

Now listen to a talk and check your answers.

Play the passage for the students to check their answers.

Answers

University Centre: art gallery, student information centre, financial aid, auditoriums, museum

Students' Union: radio station, nightclub, cinema, student newspaper

 2 Listen again and label map C. Use the words and phrases in F.

Refer the students to map C, in particular the Students' Union, University Centre, Strong, Cornett and Clearihue buildings.

Play the passage again and have the students label the map with the words and phrases in F.

Go over the answers with the class.

Answers

1 lecture halls
2 museum
3 sociology
4 humanities, student computing
5 student newspaper

➤ **Further practice:** *Achieve IELTS Workbook,* Unit 2 Vocabulary activity 1

3 Label the diagram. Use the words and phrases in G.

Direct the students to the diagram and elicit as much vocabulary as possible.

Ask the students to label the diagram with the words in G.

Answers

1 video conferencing
2 workstation
3 modem
4 wireless network
5 cluster room
6 server
7 webcam

Now work in pairs. Ask each other the questions.

Go over the questions with the students.

Put the students in pairs and have them ask each other the questions.

Get one or two answers from the class.

Open answers

➤ **Further practice:** *Achieve IELTS Workbook,* Unit 2 Vocabulary activity 2

 4 Listen to a seminar and write OU (Open University) or VC (Virtual Campus).

Explain the term Open University (a British university where students study through television, radio and short courses), and the idea of the virtual campus (where teaching would be done entirely through computers).

Tell the students that they will listen to part of a seminar and should decide which sentences are about the Open University and which are about the Virtual Campus.

Play the passage and have the students label 1–4.

Answers

1 OU   2 VC   3 VC   4 OU

5 Listen again and complete the notes. Write no more than three words for each answer.

Go over the notes with the students.

If you wish, you could ask the students to complete as much as they can from memory.

Play the passage again and ask the students to complete the notes with no more than three words for each answer.

Answers

1 Virtual Learning Environment
2 lectures
3 tutorials
4 decreases
5 their degree/course
6 the social life

Achieve IELTS: repeated information

As the students will hear the listening passages in the listening test once only, very often the answer is repeated either directly (often the case with spelling and numbers) or given again in different words. This is may be preceded by a phrase indicating that the answer will be given in a different form. The students should listen for these to be ready for the repeated answer.

Go over the explanations and examples with the students.

See if the students can give you any more ways of rephrasing.

If you wish, you could play the listening

passage again so that the students can listen for the ways of rephrasing.

Now rewrite the sentences.

Go over the sentences with the students and ask them to rewrite them.

Possible answers

1 In other words, every year the number of international students in Australia rises by 12%.
2 That is to say, there are many reasons for the choice of university, including course contents and campus types.

6 **Work in pairs. Ask each other the questions.**

Go over the questions and make sure the students understand.

Have the students ask each other the questions.

At the end of the discussion get one or two students to tell the class their answers.

Open answers

➤ **Further practice:** *Achieve IELTS Workbook,* Unit 2 Listening

Writing

Go over the IELTS tasks with the students and make sure they understand what they will learn in the section.

1 **Match the words and phrases in H with charts 1–3.**

Go over the words and phrases in H and ask the students to match them with the charts.

Answers

chart 1: increase, rise
chart 2: levelling off, remain stable
chart 3: decrease, fall, drop, reduction

2 **Complete the sentences. Use the words in I.**

Go over the words in I with the students and make sure they understand them.

Tell the students that there is more than one answer for each sentence.

Answers

1 sharp, dramatic
2 slight, gradual, slow
3 sharp, dramatic

Now underline the phrases that introduce the description.

In Unit 1 the students learnt how to refer to a table or chart. In this unit they will learn how to introduce the chart or table as a whole.

Refer the students back to the sentences in 2 and ask them to underline the phrases for introducing tables and charts.

Answers

In the first chart we can see …
As can be seen in the next chart …
As is shown in the last chart …

3 **Look at charts 4 and 5 and order the sentences.**

Refer the students to charts 4 and 5 and ask them one or two questions about them, for example 'What is chart 4 about? What is chart 5 about? How many overseas students studied in Australia in 2001? How many students from India went to Australia to study in 2003?'

Have the students order the sentences.

Answers

G B C A F D E

Now work in pairs. Ask each other the questions.

Go over the questions with the students.

Put the students in pairs and have them ask each other the questions.

At the end of the discussion get one or two answers from the students.

Open answers

4 **Look at chart 6 and write a short paragraph about student numbers in the UK.**

Go over chart 6 with the students and ask them one or two questions about it, for example 'How many students came from Asia in 1997? Why do you think the number of students from Asia fell in 1998?'

Ask the students to write a short paragraph about the graph, paying particular attention to introducing the description of the chart and the description of trends.

See page 29 for suggested answer and commentary.

➤ **Further practice:** *Achieve IELTS Workbook,* Unit 2 Reading; Unit 2 Study skills

Suggested answer

The line graph shows the number of international students studying in the UK between 1996 and 2002. The student numbers are shown in thousands and by region. As the chart shows, the overall trend is an increase in international students studying in the UK, despite a temporary drop in numbers beginning in 1997. Between 1996 and 1997 there was a sharp rise in the number of students from Asia and a slight increase in students from the other regions. However, in 1997 student numbers from Asia fell sharply, and this was followed by slight decreases in numbers from the Middle East between 1998 and 2001 and Africa between 1999 and 2000. During this period, the number of students from the United States remained steady and began to increase slightly after 2000. In fact, student numbers from most regions began to rise again after 2000. The biggest increase was in students from Asia which rose dramatically to over 12,000 in 2002 – almost double the number in 1996.

Student's answer

This line graph shows the number of overseas students from Asia, Africa, Middle East, and US in the UK from 1996 to 2002. The students from Middle East and US increased gradually over 8 years and the numbers from both countries are about 2000 in 2002. The number of students from Africa increased slightly until 1998, but after that it increased steadily and became 5000 in 2002 which is more than twice as much as that in 1996. The biggest number of students is from Asia in this period. In 1997 it declined a little, but soon it rose dramatically and it became 13000 in 2002. From this line graph it can be said that the number of overseas students in the UK will be continue to increase.

> **Comment**
> This essay shows good language control and uses a fair range of structures and vocabulary. The data is described accurately and completely. However, at 128 words, this writing is underlength, which may restrict the score to less than band 6.0.

UNIT 3
Living space

Themes types of accommodation, household chores, places in residences

Passages the effect of housework on relationships (reading); a conversation after a party, a talk about rules in a hall of residence (listening)

Language study *will* and *going to* (introduction), *must, need to, have to* (listening)

Express yourself talking about untidiness (listening)

Achieve IELTS talking about your home (speaking), task fulfilment (writing)

Vocabulary

household chores *washing up, vacuuming, ironing, washing, cooking, cleaning, making beds, DIY (do it yourself)*

renting accommodation *share, rent, landlord/landlady, flatmate/housemate*

places to live *detached house, semi-detached house, apartment block, bungalow, apartment, hall of residence, bedsit*

adjectives for accommodation *spacious, airy, cold, bright, modern, stuffy, cosy, gloomy, old-fashioned, messy, cramped, tidy*

places in residences *kitchen, bedroom, living room, dining room, bathroom, corridor, balcony, foyer, porter's lodge, canteen, laundrette*

staff in residences *receptionist, security staff, caretaker*

Background reading

Although it is increasingly common for students in Australia and Britain to live at home while studying (due to the increasing cost of education), it remains more usual for students to leave home and move to another part of the country for their higher education. During the first year at university, students usually live in university accommodation – usually halls of residence. These can be mixed or single-gender halls. Students can continue to stay in university accommodation, but

---

it is more usual for second and third year students to find rented accommodation, or digs, outside the university. Students will often share a house with other students, each having their own room and sharing the kitchen, bathroom and living room.

House share

This section introduces the unit and gives practise in listening test parts 1 and 2 and the speaking test.

1 **Name the housework in the picture. Choose from the words in A.**

Direct the students to the picture and go over the words in A.

Make sure the students understand the words, then ask them to decide which kind of housework they can see in the picture.

Answer

ironing

2 **Match the words in B with the definitions.**

Go over the words in B and the definitions.

Ask the students to match the words with the definitions.

Answers
1 flatmate or housemate
2 rent
3 landlord or landlady
4 share

3 **Do the quiz.**

Additional activity: sharing

If you wish, you could go through the introductory questions and have a brief class discussion before the students do the quiz. Other questions you could use are 'Does anyone share a flat or house? Are you easy to get on with or do you need your own space?'

Go over the quiz with the students and explain any unknown words, for example *schedule* (timetable) and *throw someone out* (to make someone leave a place).

Have the students do the quiz individually. If you wish, you could have the students compare their answers in pairs when they have finished.

Now turn to assignment 3.1 and check your results.

Ask the students to turn to assignment 3.1 and check their answers.

.18 4 **Listen to a conversation. Which jobs do the students talk about? Circle five letters A–H.**

Explain that the students will listen to a conversation between three housemates planning a party and that they should listen and decide which jobs they hear.

Go over A–H, then play the listening passage. Have the students listen and circle the jobs.

Answers

A C E F G

.18 5 **Listen again and answer the questions.**

If you wish, you could see if the students can answer the questions from the first time they listened, then play the passage again to check their answers.

Otherwise, go over the questions and play the listening passage again.

Answers

1 his assignments
2 by taxi
3 He is helping with preparations for a dance at the Students' Union.

Language study: *will* and *going to*

6 **Study the examples and explanations.**

Go over the examples and explanations with the students. If you wish, play the passage again for students to listen to the examples again.

Explain that we use *will* when we make a decision about the future at the time of speaking. We use *will* for offers and promises and also to make predictions about the future. In contrast, we use *going to* to talk about the future when we base our predictions on present evidence or intentions.

Now work in groups of three. Each student should offer to do three things on the list, then check with the group that everybody knows what they are going to do.

Go over the household jobs with the students and explain any unknown words, for example *snacks* (small pieces of food usually eaten between meals or with drinks).

Explain that they are going to have a party and need to share the jobs between them. Each student in the group should offer to do three things and give an explanation of why they would like to do it. If more than one student offers to do the same thing, the students should say why they should be chosen to do the job. When they have allocated the jobs, have the students check who is doing which job. Ask the students to use *going to* at this point.

Put the students into groups of three and have them do the activity.

➤ **Further practice:** *Achieve IELTS Workbook*, Unit 3 Language study; Unit 3 Pronunciation

Listening

Go over the IELTS tasks with the students and make sure they understand what they will learn in the section.

There are two listening passages: the first is a conversation after a party, the second is a talk about rules in a hall of residence.

1 **Work in pairs. Decide which jobs go together with *do*, *make* or *take*.**

Go over the jobs with the students and explain any unknown words, for example *recycling* (using something again).

Ask the students to decide which jobs go with which verbs, and do the first one as an example.

Put the students in pairs and have them do the activity.

Answers

do: the washing up, the cleaning, the gardening, cooking
make: the bed
take: the rubbish away, the bottles for recycling

.19 **Now listen to the conversation and tick the jobs you hear.**

Play the passage and ask the students to tick the jobs they hear.

Answers

the rubbish away ✓ the bottles for recycling ✓
washing-up ✓ cleaning ✓ cooking (Ahmed
mentions that his mother does this) ✓
tidying up ✓

 2 Listen again and circle A–D.

Explain to the students that they will listen to
a conversation after the party. They should
circle the letter that completes each sentence.

Play the listening passage and have the
students circle the letters.

Answers

1 D   2 C   3 A (he's always trying to get out
of the housework)

Express yourself: talking about untidiness

 Listen and underline the stressed words.

Go over the sentences and explain that we use
these phrases for commenting on the
(un)tidiness of a place. Make sure the students
understand all the words, for example *tip* (a
place where rubbish is left). As they will see
later in the writing section, British students are
not very good at housework, so these phrases
should be very useful if the students attend a
British university.

Play the recording and ask the students to
mark the stressed words.

Answers

<u>Look</u> at the <u>state</u> of this <u>place</u>.
<u>What</u> a <u>mess</u>.
It's <u>so</u> <u>untidy</u>.
It's an <u>absolute</u> <u>tip</u>.

Now listen again and practise.

Play the recording again. Practise the sentences
paying attention to stress and intonation.

> **Additional activity: role play**
>
> Ask the students to work in pairs and
> write a short conversation to include one
> or two of the sentences.
>
> Possible situations could be: landlord/ land-
> lady to students after a party, parents to
> children, housemates/flatmates to each other.
>
> Then have the students practise their
> dialogues and ask one or two pairs to act
> out their conversation for the class.

Language study: *must(n't), need to* and *have to*

3 Study the examples and explanations.

Go over the examples and explanations with
the students.

If you wish, play the passage again for students
to listen to the examples in context again.

Explain that must is a modal verb. It is always
followed by a verb in the bare infinitive
(infinitive without to). We use *must* for
obligation (this unit) or for strong advice (see
Unit 9). When the obligation comes from an
outside body, for example another person or a
set of rules, we tend to use *have to*. We can
only use *must* to talk about the present or the
future (*I must leave in an hour*). To talk about
the past, we use *had to*.

Need can be used as both a verb and a modal
verb. When it is used as a modal verb, like
must, it is followed by a bare infinitive and does
not carry an -s ending, has no past tense, and
questions and negatives are formed without do.
In the example and conversation, we have *need*
as an ordinary verb because the modal form of
the verb is usually used in a present situation
(usually in the negative): *We needn't worry
about the mess, the cleaner will tidy up.*

Now complete the sentences.

Go over 1–3 with the students and ask them to
complete the sentences with a suitable modal
verb.

Answers

1 must – The order is directly from the
landlord. *Have to* is also acceptable in the
sense that the rules for renting the house
include keeping it tidy, and therefore there is
the sense of indirect obligation.

2 have to – The rules for renting the house
include keeping it tidy.

3 don't need to, need to/have to – *Must* is not
correct. The correct question using *must*
would be *Must we clean the bathroom?*

**4 Work in pairs. Ask each other which jobs in
the house you have to do today.**

If you wish, you could tell the students which
household jobs they have to do.

Put the students in pairs and have them discuss
which jobs they have to do.

Go round and monitor for the correct use of
have to, must and *need to*.

Open answers

➤ **Further practice:** *Achieve IELTS Workbook,*
Unit 3 Language study activities 6 and 7

5 Put the words in C into groups.

Go over the words and phrases with the
students and ask them to put the words into
groups.

Answers

1 accommodation: hall of residence, bedsit,
  apartment
2 places in a hall: foyer, porter's lodge, dining
  hall, laundrette
3 people working in a hall: receptionist,
  security staff, caretaker, housekeeping staff

....
Additional activity: brainstorming

If you wish, you could ask the students if
they know any other words to add to the
lists.

Possible answers

accommodation: flat, dormitory,
detached house, bungalow, shared house

places in a hall: kitchen, showers,
bathroom

people working in a hall: porter, cleaner
....

1.21 **Now listen to the accommodation officer
giving a talk to new students. Tick the words
you hear.**

Play the listening passage and have the
students tick the words they hear.

Answers

All of the words in C ✓

1.21 **6 Listen again and complete the sentences.
Write no more than three words for each
space.**

Go over the notes with the students. If you
wish, you could ask the students to try to
predict what could possibly complete the
notes.

Make sure the students understand they
should write no more than three words.

Play the listening passage again and have the
students complete the notes.

Answers

1 hall of residence
2 shared
3 (TV) license

4 porter's lodge
5 laundrette
6 housekeeping
7 caretaker's
8 main receptionist
9 bedsit
10 shared house

7 Work in pairs. Ask each other the questions.

Go over the questions with the class and have
the students discuss them.

At the end of the discussion, get the answers
from one or two pairs.

Open answers

➤ **Further practice:** *Achieve IELTS Workbook,*
Unit 3 Listening; Unit 3 Vocabulary; Unit 3
Study skills

Reading

Go over the IELTS tasks with the students and
make sure they understand what they will
learn in the section.

**1 Tick who usually does these jobs in the
house.**

Go over the table with the students. If you
wish, you could ask the students for more
members of a family.

Put the students in pairs and have them
complete the table.

Open answers

Now discuss the questions.

Go over the questions with the class and have
the students discuss them.

At the end of the discussion, get the answers
from one or two pairs.

Open answers

**2 Work in pairs. Read the title of the passage
and guess the reasons for it.**

Ask the students to read the title of the
passage. Alternatively, write the title of the
passage on the board. Ask the students to
guess how and why sharing housework equally
makes a happy relationship.

If you wish, you could ask why not sharing
housework makes an unhappy relationship.

Write their predictions on the board to check
after activity 4.

Open answers

Now read the passage. Do the statements reflect the claims of the writer?

Go over the statements with the students and make sure they understand any new words, for example *depressed* (a condition in which a person's feels very unhappy and disappointed).

Ask the students to read the passage and say which statements agree or disagree with the writer and which are not given.

Answers

1 Not given.
2 Yes (line 5)
3 No (lines 16–17)
4 Yes (lines 19–20)
5 No (lines 23–24)

3 **Read the passage again and circle one letter A–D.**

Go over the questions with the students and ask them to read the passage again and circle one of the letters A–D.

Answers

1 C (line 14)
2 B (lines 7–8)
3 D (lines 15–17)

4 **Complete the summary. Choose no more than two words or a number from the reading passage for each answer.**

Ask the students to read the summary, then read the passage again and complete the summary with no more than two words for each gap.

Answers

1 women
2 men
3 equally
4 eighty percent
5 increases
6 a job
7 teamwork
8 (equally) share

5 **Match the definitions with the words in D.**

Go over the words with the students and ask them to use their dictionaries if necessary.

Have the students match the words with the definitions.

Answers

1 estimate   2 ratio   3 division   4 norm
5 remainder

6 **Make opposites with the words in E. Use these prefixes.**

Go over the prefixes with the students and ask them to make opposites using the prefixes and the words in C.

Answers

unequal, unimportant, unbalanced, inequality, unfulfilling

Note the difference between *unbalanced* (adjective) and *imbalanced* (noun).

> **Additional activity: negatives**
>
> Ask the students to think of more words with these negative prefixes.
>
> Remind the students that learning the opposite of a word is a good way of expanding their vocabulary.

7 **Look at the example and complete the chart for yourself. Use the words in F.**

Go over the words and the example with the students.

Have the students make a chart for themselves.

Open answers

Now work in pairs. Compare and discuss your charts.

Ask the students to compare and discuss their charts with a partner.

Open answers

➤ **Further practice:** *Achieve IELTS Workbook,* Unit 3 Reading

Speaking

Go over the IELTS tasks with the students and make sure they understand what they will learn in the section.

1 **Match the words in G with the pictures.**

Direct the students to the pictures. Have the students match the words with the pictures.

Answers

A semi-detached house   B detached house
C bungalow   D apartment block

Now work in pairs. Decide which is the most important feature of a house.

Go over the words and phrases with the students, then put the students into pairs or groups and have them discuss the most important feature.

If you wish, you could ask the students to give you the three most important features and the least important feature.

Open answers

2 **Describe the pictures with the words in H.**

Direct the students to the pictures.

Go over the words with the students and explain any new words, for example *stuffy* (a place with little air), *cramped* (a small space with very little room to move), *gloomy* (a place with very little light).

Suggested answers

Room A: spacious, airy, bright, modern, tidy
Room B: stuffy, gloomy, messy, cramped

Pronunciation

1.22 3 **Listen and notice how we say final -y in these words.**

Play the recording to the students and focus their attention on the pronunciation of final -y in the words.

1.22 **Now listen again and practise.**

Then play the recording again and have the students practise the words, making sure they pronounce final -y as a short sound.

1.23 4 **Listen and label the plan with the words in I.**

Direct the students to the plan.

Go over the words with the students and explain any new words, for example *corridor* (a narrow space between rooms).

Note: there are seven words and only six answers, this is because one of the rooms has two uses.

Play the listening passage and have the students label the plan.

If you wish, you could refer the students to the audioscript and have them underline any useful words and phrases, for example Let me tell you about my home. It's just right for a small family. When you enter.

Answers

1 living room and dining room
2 kitchen
3 balcony
4 corridor
5 bedrooms
6 bathroom

Achieve IELTS: talking about your home

When the examiner first meets the student, their first task is to calm the student and make them feel less nervous in order to properly assess their level. At the start of the interview, the examiner may ask one or two general or personal questions which the students can answer easily. A typical topic is about the student's home. If the student is ready for this question, they may be able to lead into the exam in a confident manner.

Go over the explanation and examples.

Now write three more questions about people's homes.

Then ask the students to write three more questions about people's homes.

Get one or two questions from the students at the end of the activity.

5 **Read the topic and make notes.**

Explain to the students that they will practise part 2 of the speaking test.

Go over the topic and explain that in the test they will have one minute to make notes on the topic. This time, if you wish, you could allow the students more time in order to give a fuller answer.

Ask the students to make notes on the topic.

Now work in pairs. Take turns to talk about the topic.

Have one student take the role of the examiner and another student take the role of the candidate.

Put the students into pairs and ask them to do the activity.

If you wish, when the students have finished, ask them to swap roles and talk about the topic again.

Writing

Go over the IELTS tasks with the students and make sure they understand what they will learn in the section.

1 **Work in pairs. Ask each other the questions.**

Go over the questions with the class and have the students discuss them.

At the end of the discussion, get the answers from one or two pairs.

Open answers

2 **Look at the chart and answer the questions.**

Direct the students to the chart and go over the questions.

Ask the students to answer the questions.

Answers
1 The chart shows the housework done by male and female students.
2 20% (80% cannot wash clothes)
3 about 18%
4 about 9%

3 **Look at the chart and read the description. Decide which information is ...**

Ask the students to decide which information in the description is wrong or inaccurate, missing or irrelevant.

Answers
1 Wrong or inaccurate: the title of the graph refers to housework only, not the ability to live away from home (which would include things like managing finances, finding accommodation, shopping and so on).
2 Missing: the percentage of females who knew how to iron clothes (33%); the percentage of males who knew how to operate a vacuum cleaner (10%)

3 Not useful or irrelevant: 'Female students have a lot more clothes than males.' 'There are many fast food outlets around the campus.' 'Vacuum cleaners use a lot of electricity.'

Achieve IELTS: task achievement

Explain to the students that a major element of part 1 of the writing test is to understand and achieve the task. Candidates are assessed on how well they have achieved the task, or in other words how well they have answered the questions. Leaving out important information, writing information that is incorrect according to the chart, table or plan, and including irrelevant information will loose marks.

Go over the questions with the students.

Explain that asking themselves these questions about the chart before they begin to write will help them to achieve the task.

Now rewrite the description in 3.

Have the students rewrite the description in 3, making sure all the information is included, that it is all accurate and that irrelevant information is not included.

See page 37 for suggested answer and commentary.

4 **Write questions about housework for the other students.**

Go over the examples with the students.

Ask the students to write five more questions to ask the other students about housework.

Now ask ten students your questions.

Remind the students to make a note of the answers they get as they will need these in the next activity.

Have the students ask the other students in the class their questions and make a note of the answers.

5 **Put the information into a chart and write a short description.**

Ask the students to use the information they collected to make a chart.

Have the students write a short description about the chart.

➤ **Further practice:** *Achieve IELTS Workbook,* Unit 3 Writing

Suggested answer

The bar chart shows the results of some students who were interviewed about their ability to do housework. The vertical axis shows the percentage of students interviewed and the horizontal axis shows the jobs done by males and females. We can see that 80% of male students did not know how to wash clothes, while the percentage of females who could not do laundry was 60%. Not many students can cook for themselves: just 10% of the males and 20% of females. The majority of female students eat fast food instead of cooking, and even more males live on fast food: almost two out of three do this. Very few male students know how to iron their clothes, but 33% of female students can iron clothes. Only 10% of male students know how to use a vacuum cleaner but 20% of females knew how to operate one.

Student's answer

The chart shows the results of some students who do housework. It also shows the difference between the between the male and female students. We can see that 80% of male students can not wash clothes while the percentage of females who can't wash clothes is 60%. Few students can cook for themselves, only 10% of the males and 20% of the females. There are many students who eat fast food which is 60% of males and 54% of females. Not many male students know how to iron their clothes, it is only 10% but 40% of female students know how to do that. 20% of females knew how to operate a vacuum cleaner an only 10% of males know how to do that.

> **Comment**
> This writing shows a fair degree of language control, but some of the information is inaccurate and it is underlength (124 words). This would probably limit the band score to 5.0.

UNIT 4
Film society

Themes student societies, meetings, the entertainment industry

Passages an article about media literacy for children (reading); a student society meeting (listening)

Language study narrative tenses (introduction), suggestions (listening)

Express yourself talking about films (introduction)

Achieve IELTS giving longer answers (speaking)

Vocabulary

types of film *thriller, horror, comedy, romantic, science fiction, martial arts, documentary, drama, biography, docudrama*

academic verbs *examine, demonstrate, consider, assume*

committee positions *committee, treasurer, secretary, events organiser*

agendas *minutes, apologies, aob, item*

approximating *roughly, nearly, almost, approximately*

fractions and percentages *half, a third, a quarter, fifty percent, twenty-five percent*

Background reading

University Students' Unions have a number of societies. A society is basically a club. Many of these societies are sports- and subject-based. Other societies depend upon the interests of the students. Typically, a Students' Union will have a film society, an international students' society, and frequently societies based upon nationality, for example a Chinese society. A society is formed by a student or group of students who must first apply to the Students' Union. If the application is successful, the society is then given a budget and a room to operate from. For international students, societies are great places to meet other students and practise language skills. Additionally, joining a society is good for the students' CVs, as it shows that they like to be involved in organising events, in teamwork, and are willing to take on responsibilities.

Let's catch a film

This section introduces the unit and gives practise in listening test parts 1 and 2 and the speaking test.

1 **Match the definitions with the words in A.**

Refer the students to the picture and ask them if they know the name of the film and what kind of film it is.

Go over the words with the students and explain that they are all types of film.

Have the students match the words with the definitions.

Answers

1 drama   2 docudrama   3 biography
4 documentary

🔊 **1.24** 2 **Listen to a conversation and answer the questions.**

Direct the students to the picture of the two people. Ask the students what the two people are talking about. Write up two or three of the students' suggestions on the board.

Go over the questions with the students.

Play the listening passage and have the students answer the questions.

If you wish, you could also refer the students to their previous predictions and see if they were correct.

Answers

1 climbers in the Andes and how they survived a fall
2 a docudrama
3 excellent, five star reviews
4 His tutor recommended it.
5 She really enjoyed it.

🔊 **1.24** 3 **Listen again and complete each sentence with no more than three words or a number.**

Go over the paragraph with the students and ask them to listen and complete it.

Play the listening passage again and have the students fill in the gaps.

Answers

1 gangs
2 the Andes
3 at 7.30
4 trailers
5 at about 7.45
6 just over 90 minutes
7 25%
8 film society members

Now circle the correct letter A–C.

Go over the multiple-choice questions with the students and have them choose the correct answers.

Answers

1 B   2 B

Express yourself: talking about films

 Listen and underline the stressed words.

Go over the phrases with the students.

Ask them to listen and underline the stressed words. Play the recording.

Answers

It's <u>really</u> <u>exciting</u>.
How <u>good</u> was <u>that</u>?
I <u>really</u> enjoyed it – it's a <u>great</u> film.

 Now listen again and practise.

Play the recording again and have the students practise the phrases, paying attention to stress and intonation.

Language study: narrative tenses

4 **Study the examples and explanations.**

Go over the examples and explanations with the students.

If you wish, play the passage again for students to listen to the examples again.

Explain that we use the past simple to refer to states and actions in the past. We use it to talk about actions that had a short duration (*Joe broke his leg*), actions with a longer duration (*how a climber survived a disastrous fall*) or repeated action (*When I was a student I went to the students' cinema every week*).

As the past continuous is often used together with the past tense to refer to a background event or to describe a situation at that time, we typically use the past continuous when we are telling a story or describing the

background to a narrative. Like all continuous tenses, we do not use the past continuous to talk about a repeated action in the past (*When I was a student I ✗ was going to the students' cinema every week*), or with stative verbs (*As they were climbing the mountain, the climbers ✗ were seeing the bad weather closing in*).

Now complete the sentences.

Refer the students to the questions and ask them to complete them with the correct form of the verbs in brackets.

Answers

1 were approaching, occurred
2 were walking, remembered
3 was walking, fell, broke
4 was lowering, went

➤ **Further practice:** *Achieve IELTS Workbook,* Unit 4 Listening; Unit 4 Language study activity 1

5 **Work in pairs. Ask each other the questions.**

Go over the questions with the class then have the students discuss them.

Make sure that for question 3 the students are using narrative tenses correctly.

At the end of the discussion, get the answers from one or two pairs.

Open answers

Reading

Go over the IELTS tasks with the students and make sure they understand what they will learn in the section.

> **Background reading**
> Media studies has become increasingly popular with students in the UK, many preferring to take it in preference to the more traditional subjects. However, some people used to see media studies as a 'soft' subject as opposed to subjects like physics, mathematics and languages.

1 **Work in pairs. Answer the questions.**

Go over the questions with the class then have the students discuss them.

At the end of the discussion, get the answers from one or two pairs.

Answers

1 Open answers. The students will check their answers to this question in the next part.
2 Suggested answer – The media is increasingly important in people's lives and as an industry.
3 Open answers.

Now read the passage and check your answers to question 1.

Ask the students to read the passage and check their answers to question 1 only.

Answer

They study public communications such as film, newspapers, adverts, music and videos. They consider definitions of *culture* and *media* and look at cultural material, the way culture shapes people's values and beliefs and the way media and institutions transmit ideas and values.

> **Additional activity: Latin words in academic English**
>
> Explain to the students that *media* is a word from Latin and therefore has irregular singular and plural forms. The singular is *medium*, the plural is *media*.
>
> Explain the meaning of *curriculum*, *fungus*, and *criterion*. Then ask the students to find the plurals in their dictionary.
>
> **Answers**
>
> curriculum *curricula*,   fungus *fungi*, criterion *criteria*

2 **Find the words in B in the text and choose the definition.**

Ask the students to read the text again and find the words in B.

Ask the students to try to get the correct definition for the words.

Answers

1 consider   2 demonstrate   3 examine
4 assume

3 **Read the passage in 1 again. Write ...**

Go over the 'true', 'false', 'not given' statements with the students.

Ask them to read the passage again and decide which statements are true, false or not given.

Answers

1 True – 'we consider competing definitions'
2 False – 'a range of cultural material from a variety of media'
3 True – 'While we assume that the meaning of much of the cultural material around us is obvious and transparent, this course demonstrates that we are constantly interpreting and decoding'
4 Not given
5 False – 'the importance of brands and fashion'

4 **Work in pairs. Ask each other the questions.**

Go over the questions with the class then have the students discuss them.

At the end of the discussion, get the answers from one or two pairs.

Open answers

5 **Read passage and choose the most suitable title A–E.**

Go over the titles with the students.

Direct the students to the picture and ask them what they think the passage is about.

Have them read the whole of the reading passage and choose the most suitable title.

Answer

A Media studies for children

6 **Read the passage again and circle the appropriate letters A–D.**

Go over the multiple-choice questions with the students.

Have them read the passage again and choose the correct answers.

You may like to explain *watching the box* (colloquial for watching TV), *cookies* (American English for biscuits, also biscuits with pieces of chocolate in them), *commercial break* (TV advertisements shown during a pause in the main programming), *get their message across* (sell their product to people).

Answers

1 B – 'children as young as three may be learning in the most basic way the sort of skills that are taught on such courses' (lines 6–8)
2 A – 'Although product placement is banned for programme makers in Britain, on commercial TV as well as the BBC' (lines 27–28)

3 D – 'With the rise of digital TV which enables viewers to skip commercial breaks, some experts say advertisers might need to be increasingly creative about ways to get their message across' (lines 47–52)

4 A – 'the British Film Institute's Cary Bazalgette rejects the term *media studies* in favour of *media literacy*' (lines 63–65)

7 Read the statements and tick the ones you agree with.

Go over the questions with the students and have them tick the statements they agree with. Encourage them to note one or two reasons why they support the statement.

Open answers

Now work in pairs. Discuss and give reasons for your answers.

Ask the students to discuss the statements and put them into pairs, or if you wish, groups.

At the end of the discussion, get the answers from one or two pairs.

Open answers

➤ **Further practice:** *Achieve IELTS Workbook*, Unit 4 Reading

Listening

Go over the IELTS tasks with the students and make sure they understand what they will learn in the section.

The listening passage is a student society meeting. It is split into three parts: going over the agenda (activities 3–5), item 1 – the equipment (activities 6–7), item 2 – suggestions for the film society film night (activities 8–9).

1 Work in pairs. Answer the questions.

Go over the questions with the class then have the students discuss them.

At the end of the discussion, get the answers from one or two pairs.

Open answers

2 Match the words with the definitions.

Go over the words with the students and explain that they are all words used to describe parts of a meeting.

Have the students match the words and definitions.

Answers

1 c   2 d   3 b   4 a

3 Put the agenda items in 2 in order.

Explain *agenda* (the plan of a meeting) to the students.

Ask the students to put the stages of the agenda in order and explain that they will check their answers in the next stage of the activity.

 Now listen to a meeting and check your answers.

Play the listening passage and have the students check their answers to activity 3.

Answers

1 apologies   2 minutes   3 items   4 aob

4 Label the diagram. Use the words in C.

Go over the words with the students and explain that they are mostly positions in a committee.

Have the students label the diagram.

Answers

1 committee   2 treasurer   3 secretary
4 events organiser

1.26 5 Listen again. Complete the agenda.

Play the listening passage again and ask the students to complete the agenda.

Answers

1 apologies, he has to finish an assignment, he is ill
2 approved: YES, objections: NO
3 the equipment, film night

➤ **Further practice:** *Achieve IELTS Workbook*, Unit 4 Vocabulary

6 Label the picture. Use the words in D.

Direct the students to the picture and refer them to the words in box D.

Ask them to label the picture with the words, using their dictionaries if necessary.

Answers

A sound system   B projector   C film
D screen   E seats

1.27 Now listen and tick the things you hear.

✓ screen ✓ projector ✓ film

1.27 7 Listen again. Circle three letters A–E.

Go over 1 and 2 with the students.

Play the listening passage and have the students circle the letters.

Answers

1 B, C, E
2 £1,500, £1,300

8 Label the pictures. Choose from the words in E.

Direct the students to the pictures and elicit what kind of films they are.

Go over the types of film and explain any new words.

Have the students choose three of the film types and match them with the pictures.

Answers

1 thriller   2 martial arts   3 science fiction

1.28 Now listen and circle the correct letters A–C.

Play the listening passage and have the students choose the correct letter.

1 B   2 C   3 B

9 Match the verbs with the nouns.

Go over the verbs and nouns and explain any new words.

Ask the students to match the verbs with the nouns.

Answers

1 d   2 e   3 b   4 a   5 c

Language study: suggestions

10 Study the examples and explanations.

Go over the examples and explanations with the students.

If you wish, play the passage again for students to listen to the examples again.

Explain that we use suggestions to offer alternatives to other people. Explain to the students that we usually give a reason for rejecting a suggestion, it is not enough to just say no.

Now complete the sentences.

Ask the students to complete the sentences with a word or phrase from 10.

Answers

1 Your thoughts on this/Any suggestions about this
2 like to suggest
3 How about
4 avoid doing that

1.29 11 Listen and check your answers.

Play the recording and have the students check their answers.

➤ **Further practice:** *Achieve IELTS Workbook*, Unit 4 Listening activity 2

Pronunciation

1.29 12 Listen again and practise.

Play the recording again and ask the students to practise the sentences paying attention to stress and intonation.

13 Work in pairs. Student A, you are the President of the Film Society – read your role card. Student B, you are the Events Organiser – read your role card.

Tell the students that they are going to practise making suggestions and rejecting and offering alternative suggestions.

Split the class into two groups – Students A and Students B – and ask them to look at their assignment role cards.

Give them one or two minutes to prepare what they are going to say.

Now have a conversation using the role cards.

Put the students into pairs and have them practise the conversation.

If you wish, you could ask one or two pairs to show their conversation to the class.

➤ **Further practice:** *Achieve IELTS Workbook*, Unit 4 Listening

Speaking

Go over the IELTS tasks with the students and make sure they understand what they will learn in the section.

The first activity is an extension of the listening section, but can be done as it stands.

1 Work in groups. Discuss ways to raise funds for a new piece of equipment for a student society. Follow these steps.

Tell the students that they are going to hold their own meeting.

The meeting could be for the film society or another society connected to your school. Whatever you or the students decide, they have to discuss ways of raising money for a new piece of equipment.

Ask the students to decide on a club or society name and an agenda (or, alternatively, write an agenda for the students yourself). Ask them to appoint a chairperson, treasurer and secretary and any other positions they think the committee needs.

Tell the students to hold their meeting and make sure they come up with definite points of action for each of their items.

Put the students into groups of three or four and ask them to hold their own meeting.

If you wish, you could ask the secretary to take minutes of the meeting, then tell the class the results of the meeting.

2 **Read the topic below and underline the main points.**

Go over the topic with the students and ask them to underline the main points. The students will be asked to do this repeatedly throughout *Achieve IELTS* to get them into the practise of identifying the main and most important points.

Ask the students what they think are the most important points and write one or two on the board.

Suggested answer

Part 2: Describe a film you saw which made an impression on you.

You should say:
1 what film and what type of film it is
2 when you saw it
3 what your favourite part of the film is

and explain why it made an impression on you.

Now make notes on the main points.

Ask the students to make one or two short notes on the main points. This reproduces test procedure and prepares them for the final speaking activity.

Open answers

.30 3 **Read the notes, then listen and write ∧ when you hear any extra information.**

Ask the students to read the notes.

Explain that on the recording they will hear extra information and they should mark ∧ where they hear this.

Play the recording and have the students mark where they hear the extra information.

If you wish, you could play the recording again, pausing after each answer and ask the students to write the extra information.

Answers (underlined)

My favourite film is the Matrix <u>because it is such a fast-moving film</u>. It's a science fiction film <u>but at the same time you could call it an action film</u>. I saw it a few years ago, as soon as it was released, <u>in fact I was the first one of my friends to see it</u>. The best part of the film was when the main character was trying to rescue his friend. <u>I like this part because the special effects are amazing</u>. It made a big impression on me <u>as it was technically so far ahead of any other film at that time</u> – I liked it very much.

Achieve IELTS: giving longer answers

The individual long turn is where the students have the chance to develop the ideas in the topic and show the examiner their range of vocabulary and fluency. A short answer will mean that the examiner has to ask further questions in order make an assessment. It is much better if the students are able to develop their answers by giving more details and reasons, as in the recording in activity 3.

Go over the phrases for giving longer answers with the students.

Then ask the students to go back to the notes they made for the topic in activity 2 and see if they can use the phrases to give longer answers.

4 **Work in pairs. Discuss the topic in activity 2.**

Put the students into pairs and ask them to discuss the topic in 2.

Have one student take the role of the examiner and the other student take the role of the candidate.

If you wish, when the students have finished, ask them to swap roles and talk about the topic again.

Writing

Go over the IELTS tasks with the students and make sure they understand what they will learn in the section.

1 Match the numbers with the words.

Go over the numbers with the students and ask them to match the numbers with the phrases.

Answers

1 c   2 d   3 b   4 a

> **Background reading**
>
> In American English, *a billion* means a thousand million. In British English, *a billion* means a million million (although a thousand million is becoming a more common definition in British English).

Additional activity: pronouncing large numbers

If you wish, you could have the students practise the pronunciation of large numbers.

Model the pronunciation for the students and have them practise.

➤ **Further practice:** *Achieve IELTS Workbook*, Unit 4 Pronunciation

Now match the numbers with films a–d.

Explain the table to the students, which is a selection of the top-earning (in other words, biggest grossing) films worldwide to 2004.

Ask the students to look at the table and match the figures with the films.

Answers

1 a   2 c   3 d   4 b

2 Look at the chart and answer the questions.

Go over the questions with the students and ask them to look at the table and find the answers.

Answers

1 *Lord of the Rings Return of the King*
2 *Jurassic Park, Lord of the Rings the Two Towers, Harry Potter, Star Wars Episode 1*

Now work in pairs. Ask each other the questions.

Go over the questions with the students. Put the students in pairs and ask them to discuss the questions.

Open answers

3 Label the charts. Use the words in F.

Ask the students to look at the charts and match the words with the charts.

Answers

1 a quarter   2 a half   3 a third   4 a fifth

Now make sentences.

Ask the students to use the chart in activity 1 and make sentences with the word and phrases in the table.

Possible answers

Forrest Gump took approximately a third of the amount of money of *Titanic*.

Jurassic Park took nearly half of the amount of money of *Titanic*.

Star Wars, Episode 1 took roughly half of the amount of money of *Titanic*.

1.31 4 Listen to a talk and complete the passage.

Ask the students one or two lead in questions, for example 'Which country makes the most films? Which country is the second biggest film producer?' Then ask the students to read the passage and find out.

Have the students listen to the passage and complete it.

Answers

1 by far	2 over 700
3 slightly over half	4 at almost 400
5 nearly 300	6 over 100

Now circle the phrases for referring to figures.

Ask the students to read the talk again and underline the phrases for referring to figures.

Answers

by far   over   slightly over   at almost   nearly   just over

5 Look at the chart in activity 1 and write a paragraph.

See page 45 for suggested answer and commentary.

➤ **Further practice:** *Achieve IELTS Workbook*, Unit 4 Writing; Unit 4 Study skills

Suggested answer

The bar chart shows a selection of the biggest grossing (or earning) films, up to 2004 in billions of dollars and by the date of release. The biggest grossing film of all time up to 2004 was *Titanic*, released in 1997, which took over $1.8 billion – almost 50% more than the next biggest grossing film, *The Lord of the Rings*. The next four biggest grossing films took roughly the same amount, earning between nine hundred million and one billion dollars. Following this, released in 2003, *Finding Nemo* took just over half the amount of the biggest grossing film and *Forrest Gump* took over a third of the amount. Interestingly, the oldest film, *Jaws*, released in 1975 managed to take four hundred and seventy million, six hundred thousand dollars – almost a quarter of the amount taken by Titanic.

Student's answer

In the graph is describing grossing films to 2004. First, the biggest grossing films is Titanic during 1997, the grossing was over $1.8 billion. Secondly, that is The Lord of the Rings; the Return of the King in 2003, the grossing was more than $1 billion. Thirdly, that is Harry Potter and the Philosopher's Stone in 2001, the grossing was near to $1 billion. And the Star Wars Episode 1 in 1999; the Lord of the Rings, the Two Towers in 2002 and Jurassic Park in 1993 are all a little less than Harry Potter and the Philosopher's Stone; and this three films haven't a big disparity of grossing. Finding Nemo in 2003, the grossing was more than $0.8 billion. The eighthly is Forrest Gump in 1994, the grossing was near to $0.7 billion. The last one is Jaws in 1975; the grossing was near to $0.5 billion. This graph is how the grossing of top 9th films to 2004.

> **Comment**
> This essay shows good language control and uses a fair range of structures and vocabulary. The data is described accurately and completely. However, at 128 words, this writing is underlength, which may restrict the score to less than band 6.0.

UNIT 5
Bulletin

Themes student radio station, new bulletins, international news agencies

Passages a description about a news agency (reading); news bulletins, international news agencies (listening)

Language study present perfect for experiences (introduction), present perfect for recent events (listening), giving reasons

Express yourself personal information (introduction)

Achieve IELTS reading for general understanding (reading)

Vocabulary

news and news agencies *syndicate, press, corporation, co-operative, agency, broadcasting, cable, network*

information technology *data, website, database, download, statistics*

Background reading

Many universities and colleges have their own media, in particular a student radio station, a student magazine and sometimes a student newspaper. These are run by student volunteers for other students. If a student has a particular interest in music and would like to share this with other students, they can become a DJ (disc jockey) at the radio station and broadcast their music. The title of the introduction, CUe FM is the name of the student radio at the University of Canberra, Australia.

This unit also looks at news agencies, in particular Reuters, which sell news to broadcasters and newspapers. The largest news agency is the Associated Press in America, which is a co-operative organisation jointly owned by American newspapers and broadcasters.

CUe FM

1 Work in pairs. Ask each other these questions.

Go over the questions with the students and explain any new words, for example *kettle* (an electrical appliance for boiling water), *chat-show* (two or more people on TV or radio having a light conversation), *chart music* (pop music).

Put the students in pairs and have them ask each other the quiz questions.

At the end of the discussion, get the answers from one or two pairs.

Open answers

2 Read the passage on the following page and answer the questions.

Go over the questions with the students and refer them to the passage.

Ask the students to read the passage and answer the questions.

Answers

1 the University of Canberra's (student) radio station
2 24 hours a day
3 music, news, phone-ins, gossip, discussions and competitions
4 join the CUe FM club, and pay AU$10

If you wish, you could also ask the students which kinds of music the radio broadcasts: punk, pop, rock, Australian, metal, dance, funk, blues, world music.

Background reading

Punk (rock) is a kind of music from the late 1970s with basic rhythms and short, loud songs. *Metal* is short for *heavy metal* and is characterised by loud music with long guitar solos. *Funk* is American dance music with a heavy bass line. *World music* is folk music from different parts of the world.

Now work in pairs. Answer the questions.

Go over the questions with the class and have the students discuss them.

At the end of the discussion, get the answers from one or two pairs.

Open answers

1.32 3 Listen and complete the notes. Write no more than three words or a number for each answer.

Refer the students to the form. Explain that *Tech support* (number 5) means *technical support*, that is, dealing with problems with the equipment.

Play the listening passage and ask the students to complete the form with no more than three words or a number each time.

Answers
1 IMC (Imaging and Media Communications)
2 DJ
3 UC 00579
4 interested in music
5 DJ: NO
6 Tech support: YES
7 24–3

1.32 4 Listen again and complete the notes. Write no more than three words for each answer.

Play the listening passage again and ask the students to complete the notes.

Answers
1 phone-in
2 world music
3 new items
4 competitions
5 reviews of concerts
6 phone-in slots

Express yourself: personal information

1.33 Listen and mark the stressed words.

Go over the phrases with the students and explain that these are ways of giving and asking for personal information.

Have the students listen and underline the stressed words.

Answers
… <u>tell</u> me <u>something</u> about <u>yourself</u>
Well as you <u>probably</u> <u>know</u> …
… <u>let</u> me <u>tell</u> you a bit about…

1.33 Now listen again and practise.

Play the recording again and have the students practise, paying attention to stress and intonation.

Language study: present perfect (1)

5 Study the examples and explanations.

Go over the examples and explanations with the students.

If you wish, play the passage again for students to listen to the examples in context again.

Explain that we use the present perfect to talk about a number of different situations, but that the present perfect is a way of talking about the present situation with reference to the past.

In this language study we look at the present perfect to talk about a period of time up to the present when we may not know the length of time. A typical use is for talking about experience. We can use adverbs of time to talk about the period in general terms: *always, never, recently, yet, just,* but not normally with specific periods of time: *last week, on Wednesday.* To talk about periods of time we use *since* with specific dates (*I've been here since 2 o'clock*) and *for* with length of time (*She's had the essay for three days*).

Now write the questions in full.

Answers
1 Have you ever wanted to be a DJ?
2 Have you ever listened to classical music?
3 Have you ever been to the opera?
4 Have you ever been to a pop concert?
5 Have you ever wanted to play a musical instrument?
6 Have you ever sung for people?

6 Work in pairs. Ask and answer the questions.

Put the students in pairs and have them ask each other the questions.

At the end of the discussion, get the answers from one or two pairs.

Open answers

Listening

Go over the IELTS tasks with the students and make sure they understand what they will practise in this section.

1 Match the headlines with the pictures.

Direct the students to the pictures and ask them to match the headlines with the pictures.

If you wish, you could ask one or two students to describe the pictures.

Answers

A 2 B 3 C 1

Now work in pairs. Discuss what the stories are about.

Put the students in pairs and ask them to discuss what they know about the stories in the pictures or what they think the stories are about.

This activity practises prediction skills and helps the students to engage with the listening passage.

 ## 2 Listen to a news report and order the pictures in activity 1.

Play the listening passage and ask the students to number the pictures in activity 1 according to the order they hear them in the listening passage.

Answers

B A C

 ### Now listen again and complete the notes. Write no more than three words or a number.

Go over the notes with the students and ask them to listen and fill in the gaps with no more than three words or a number.

Play the listening passage again and have the students complete the notes.

Answers

1 three times
2 12,000 years
3 in 1930
4 a comet/a planetoid
5 Korean Train Express
6 four hours
7 180,000 passengers
8 a fifth
9 third largest
10 Internet

3 Work in pairs. Discuss the questions.

Go over the questions with the class and have the students discuss them.

At the end of the discussion, get the answers from one or two pairs.

Open answers

Language study: present perfect (2)

4 Study the examples and explanations.

Go over the examples and explanations with the students.

If you wish, play the passage again for students to listen to the examples in context again.

In this language study we look at the present perfect for events in the recent past which have finished but which have an on-going importance in the present time. Typically, this is used in news stories where the story may be introduced with the present perfect and the details will be given using the past tense.

Now write full sentences for the headlines in 1 and give more details about each story.

Refer the students back to the stories in activity 1 and ask them to write full sentences for the headlines and add any more information they can remember.

Possible answers

1 Scientists have found a new planet. It is the most distant object discovered so far. Some scientists have said that it is a comet.
2 South Korea has launched a high-speed rail service. It is the fifth country to do this. It cost $15.3 billion and took 12 years.
3 A music company has cut 1,500 jobs. It is the third biggest music company in the world. It wanted to save £50 million.

Additional activity: news story

If you wish, you may like to ask the students to produce their own news report.

Put the students into small groups and ask them to decide on an important recent event to report on.

Have the students use the present perfect for the headline and the past tense to give more details about the story.

If you wish, you could ask one member of the group to be the newscaster and give the new report to the rest of the class.

➤ **Further practice:** *Achieve IELTS Workbook,* Unit 5 Language study activities 1 and 2

5 **Match the words with the definitions.**

Go over the words with the students and explain that they are all related to the news and news agencies.

Have the students match the words and definitions.

Answers

1 d   2 b   3 e   4 a   5 c

1.35 6 **Listen and circle the correct letter A–C.**

Go over the multiple-choice questions with the students.

Play the listening passage and have the students choose the correct answers.

Answers

1 B   2 B   3 B

Now write LO for large organisation, GA for government agency, CO for co-operative, or C for corporation.

Go over 1–4 with the students and see if they can classify any of the organisations from memory.

Answers

1 LO   2 CO   3 C   4 GA

1.35 7 **Listen to the seminar again and complete the table.**

Play the listening passage again and have the students complete the table.

Answers

1 41 international
2 1945
3 1,000
4 1851
5 2,000 journalists
6 1925
7 65,000 journalists

8 **Work in pairs. Discuss the questions.**

Go over the questions with the class and have the students discuss them.

At the end of the discussion, get the answers from one or two pairs.

Open answers

Reading

Go over the IELTS tasks with the students and make sure they understand what they will practise in this section.

1 **Order pictures A–D.**

Direct the students to the pictures and ask them to put the pictures in order.

Tell them that they will check their answers in the next activity.

Now read the passage and check your answers.

Ask the students to read the passage quickly and check their answers.

Answers

D   A   C   B

2 **Read the passage again. Which paragraphs state the following information?**

Ask the students to read the passage again and decide which paragraphs contain the information.

Answers

1 C (line 17)   2 D (lines 23–24)   3 A (lines 4–5)   4 E (line 36)   5 B (lines 7–8)

Now circle the correct letters A–C.

Go over the multiple-choice questions with the students and have them choose the correct answers.

They can do this from memory, or you may wish to refer them back to the reading passage again.

Answers

1 B (lines 3–4)   2 C (line 12)   3 B (line 16)
4 B (lines 24–25)   5 A (line 33)

Achieve IELTS: reading for general understanding

IELTS frequently tests the students' ability to read for general understanding, or *scanning*. The students are asked to look for the main ideas which relate to the questions. A frequent test is matching the headings with the paragraphs, but there are also questions in which students match a summary with a paragraph. Students need to practise identifying topic sentences in passages. Putting the main idea of a paragraph into their own words will help them to either choose the correct summary or heading or reject any summaries or headings that are distractors.

Go over the examples and explanations with the students.

Now underline the main ideas and key words in the passage.

Ask the students to read the passage again and underline the main ideas and key words.

For weaker classes, you may wish to use the suggested answers as part of a matching activity.

Possible answers

A 'Although it is better known as a press agency, Reuters in fact makes most of its profits through financial information.'

B 'The history of Reuters goes hand in hand with improvements in communication technology.'

C 'As overland and undersea cables were laid, Reuter's business expanded to the Far East in 1872 and South America in 1874.'

D 'the company was restructured in 1941 in order to maintain its independence as a press agency'

E 'Today's Reuters is still based on their *Trust Principles*.'

3   Work in pairs. Discuss possible headings for each paragraph.

Put the students into pairs and ask them to do the activity. This practises summarising skills and helps the students with matching headings with paragraphs.

Possible answers

A Reuters worldwide/A global news agency
B The history of Reuters
C Expansion of the business
D Company restructuring/An independent agency
E News based on fact/Into the electronic age

4   Work in pairs. Discuss the questions.

Go over the questions with the class and have the students discuss them.

At the end of the discussion, get the answers from one or two pairs.

Open answers

➤ **Further practice:** *Achieve IELTS Workbook*, Unit 5 Reading; Unit 5 Listening

Speaking

Go over the IELTS tasks with the students and make sure they understand what they will practise in this section.

1   Write the acronyms in full. Use some of the words in A.

Explain that an *acronym* is a word made out of the initial letters of several words.

Ask the students to use the words in A to complete the acronyms.

Tell them they will need one word more than once.

Answers

1 British Broadcasting Corporation
2 Cable News Network
3 Australian Broadcasting Corporation

> **Additional activity: acronym quiz**
>
> If you wish, you could ask the students for more acronyms.
>
> Alternatively, you could organise a quick team game by splitting the class into groups and asking them to say the full version of common acronyms, for example, NATO (North Atlantic Treaty Organisation), UN (United Nations), WHO (World Health Organisation), and so on.
>
> For each one a team gets correct, give them one point.

**Now work in groups. Design a schedule for a
college or local radio station. Follow these
steps.**

Put the students into groups and have them
do the activity.

At the end of the activity, get the schedule
from one or two groups, or ask the groups to
swap schedules with each other.

2 **Work in pairs. Ask each other these
questions.**

Go over the questions with the class and have
the students discuss them.

At the end of the discussion, get the answers
from one or two pairs.

Open answers

3 **Read the topic below and make notes.**

Ask the students to read the topic and make
notes.

Give them a few minutes to do this and
explain that in the exam they will only have
one minute to make notes.

**Now answer the questions and expand your
notes.**

Go over the questions with the class and have
the students answer them in order to expand
their notes.

Open answers

4 **Work in pairs. Discuss the topic.**

Put the students into pairs and ask them to do
the activity.

Have one student take the role of the
examiner and the other student take the role
of the candidate.

If you wish, when the students have finished,
ask them to swap roles and talk about the
topic again.

Writing

Go over the IELTS tasks with the students and
make sure they understand what they will
practise in this section.

1 **Work in pairs. Answer the questions.**

Go over the questions with the class and have
the students discuss them.

At the end of the discussion, get the answers
from one or two pairs.

Open answers

2 **Match the words with the definitions.**

Go over the words with the students and
explain that they are all connected to
information technology.

Have the students match the words and
definitions.

Answers

1 d   2 a   3 c   4 b

3 **Read the passage and complete the chart.**

Ask the students to read the passage and
complete the chart.

Answers

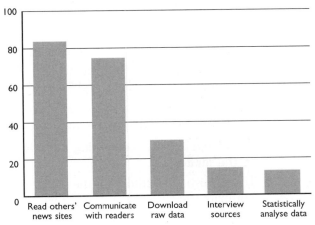

Language study: giving reasons

4 **Study the examples and explanation.**

Go over the examples and explanations with
the students.

Explain that we can use these phrases to
introduce a reason. When we want to talk
about possible causes and explanations we use
is + because (of) / caused by / the result of.

Now work in pairs. Give possible reasons for the sentences.

Go over the sentences with the students and have them think of possible reasons.

Ask the students to write their answers down using phrases for giving reasons.

Possible answers

1 A reason for this could be the growing use of information technology.
2 This could be caused by newspapers reporting news with a political preference.
3 A possible reason for this is that newspapers and broadcasters only take journalists with degrees.
4 A possible reason for this is greater experience of unfair and biased reporting.
5 A possible reason could be the high cost of gathering news.

➤ **Further practice:** *Achieve IELTS Workbook,* Unit 5 Language study activity 3

5 **Look at the table and underline the most important information.**

Direct the students to the table and ask them to underline the most important information.

Explain that they should do this when they do task 1 in the test.

Now work in pairs. Think of reasons for this.

Put the students in pairs and have them brainstorm possible reasons for the significant information in preparation for task 6.

Open answers

....

Additional activity: comparing attitudes to the media

If you wish, you could ask the students to compare the attitudes in the US with attitudes in your own country and see if there are any significant differences or similarities.

....

Achieve IELTS: giving supporting information

In answering task 1 the student is expected to describe the table, chart or information as fully as possible. This includes referring to the information given and using it in the answer. In task 1, students do not need to give their own opinions about the information or speculate about the possible causes or reasons; they do not need to refer to their own countries or comment on the information. If the student does this, he or she will not lose points, but given the limited amount of time and words they are allowed, this could mean that the students lose marks indirectly by becoming sidetracked.

Point out that when the information in the chart is not absolutely clear, they can use phrases for giving approximate figures. They can also use these to add variety to their writing.

Now read the passage in activity 3 again and find ways of referring to numbers and figures in a general way.

Refer the students back to the passage in activity 2 and ask them to read though it quickly and underline any phrases for referring to figures in a general way.

Answers

more than   eight in ten   about   at least   nearly   only

➤ **Further practice:** *Achieve IELTS Workbook,* Unit 5 Writing; Unit 5 Study skills

6 **Write a report for a university lecturer describing the information shown in activity 5. You should write at least 150 words.**

See page 53 for suggested answer and commentary.

Suggested answer

The table shows why people in America do not watch the news as often as they used to. The chart is divided into age groups and the reasons they give for not watching the news. Most young adults aged between 18 and 29 said they were too busy or did not have enough time. This figure decreases with age: 50% of 30–49 year-olds said they did not have time. In contrast with the other groups, only 21% of the oldest group said they did not have enough time. For this group, their main reason for not watching is that they are critical of the news coverage – that is, they do not believe the news is balanced or fair. This could be because they do not trust journalists and broadcasters. Interestingly, 15% of this group also reported that they had no interest in the news and a further 15% said they got their news from other sources, such as the Internet.

Student's answer

The table shows the reasons people give for watching network nightly news less often. As we can see from the table, the main trend is that the majority of young people have not time or are too bus to watch nightly news, while lots of old people are critical of average the news. A possible reason for this is young people don't care about what's new, also they have lots more things to do for fun or for work, such as date and assignment. And old people have much more experience so that they don't trust. That is interesting that the biggest number of people who don't have TV are adults. This may be caused by their busy work or financial problem, for instance, they need to pay for car, house, insurance, children education, etc. so they don't need a TV.

Comment

Although the writing fulfils the task and the information is accurate, the language used is rather repetitive and the range of vocabulary is limited. There are a lot of minor grammatical errors. This essay may be awarded band 5.0.

UNIT 6
Energy

Themes fieldwork, renewable energy, energy conservation

Passages an article on hydroelectricity (reading); a talk about the centre for sustainable energy, a lecture on solar power (listening)

Language study information questions (introduction), present passive (reading), sequence and purpose (writing),

Express yourself free time (introduction)

Achieve IELTS predicting (reading)

Vocabulary

research and verbs for academic activities *break, report, handout, field work, slide, deadline, set, hand in, lead, show, prepare, take, do*

departmental jobs *research assistant, professor, administrator, receptionist*

energy generation *reservoir, dam, head, reversible pump, penstock, turbine, outflow, power lines, transformer, intake, shaft, gearbox, blade, transformer, nacelle, hub*

energy/fuel types hydroelectric, solar, nuclear, coal, geothermal, gas, wave, oil, wind

---

Background reading

Part of many students' coursework, particularly in subjects like archaeology and geography, is fieldwork. During fieldwork, students are give a project or title that requires work away from the university, usually at an outside location for the purposes of research.

This unit covers sustainable energy generation – hydropower, biomass, fuel cells, wind power, wave power, solar energy – an increasingly important topic due to the need to reduce the effect of global warming by moving to renewable fuel sources.

Fieldwork

1 **Look at map A and decide where you would like to visit.**

Direct the students to the map of Wales and the places illustrated.

Ask the students to decide where they would like to visit and why.

Open answers

Background reading

Wales is part of the United Kingdom, but has it's own parliament (with limited domestic powers but not law-making powers). It was conquered by the English king Edward 1 in 1282 and governed from London until 1999. The country is governed from Cardiff, the capital of Wales. Wales has its own language, Welsh (a branch of Gaelic), and its official languages are English and Welsh. Many town names have English and Welsh alternative forms, for example Newtown = Drenewydd, and students will also hear Machynlleth/mækənləθ/ – the home of the Centre for Alternative Technology and ancient capital of Wales.

The Centre for Alternative Technology was set up in the mid-1970s to 'inspire, inform, and enable people to live more sustainably'. The centre tries to develop practical ways of energy conservation and generation, waste management, and recycling.

Now work in pairs. Compare your answers.

Ask the students to discuss their answers. Put the students in pairs to compare their answers.

Open answers

 2 **Listen to a conversation and tick the places you hear.**

Tell the students they will listen to two students discussing a fieldwork project, and they should tick the places the students plan to visit.

Play the listening passage and have students tick the places they hear.

Answers

✓ Snowdon   ✓ Dinorwig Electric Mountain
✓ the Centre for Alternative Technology
✓ National Botanical Gardens

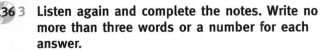 **3 Listen again and complete the notes. Write no more than three words or a number for each answer.**

Go over the table with the students and ask them to listen and complete it.

Play the listening passage again and have the students complete the table with no more than three words for each answer.

Answers

1 sustainable energy development
2 2,500
3 20 minutes seminar
4 north and mid
5 National Park
6 power station
7 alternative technology
8 preparation for presentation

Now circle the correct letter A–C.

Go over the multiple-choice questions with the students.

Have the students choose the correct answers. If you wish, you could play the listening passage again for the students to check their answers.

Answers

1 B   2 B   3 B

Express yourself: free time

1.37 Listen and underline the weak syllables.

Go over the phrases and explain that we can use these to talk about what we are doing with our free time.

Ask the students to listen and underline the weak syllables.

Answers

he's <u>at</u> a loose end
he want<u>ed</u> <u>to</u> <u>tag</u> <u>a</u>long
he's got s<u>o</u>me time <u>on</u> <u>his</u> hands

Now match the phrases with the definitions.

Ask the students to match the phrases with the meanings.

Answers

1 he's got some time on his hands
2 he's at a loose end
3 he wanted to tag along

4 Match the words in A with the definitions.

Go over the words with the students and explain that they are about academic work.

Have the students match the words and definitions.

Answers

1 fieldwork   2 report   3 break   4 slide
5 handout   6 deadline

Now match the words in A with these verbs.

Go over the verbs with the students and explain that they are connected with academic work.

Have the students match the words and definitions.

Answers

set a deadline
hand in a report
show a slide
prepare a handout (or slide)
take a break
do fieldwork

➤ **Further practice:** *Achieve IELTS Workbook,* Unit 6 Vocabulary activity 1

5 Work in pairs. Ask each other the questions.

Go over the questions with the students.

Put the students in pairs and have them discuss the questions.

At the end of the discussion, get the answers from one or two from pairs.

Open answers

Additional activity: planning a trip

Ask the students to decide which places they would like to visit in Wales. If there is time, you may want to ask the students to do further research on places to visit and things to do in Wales.

Have them decide in which order they would like to visit them, how long they would like to stay there and on which days they would go.

---

6 Work in pairs. Look at the picture and answer the questions.

Direct the students to the picture and ask them to discuss the questions. Put the students in pairs. Do not worry about use of the passive at this point as this will receive detailed attention in the Reading section.

At the end of the discussion, get the answers from one or two pairs.

Answers

1 It is a hydroelectric power station built inside a mountain.
2 When electricity is needed, water is released from the top reservoir through the turbines to generate electricity. When the water reaches the lower reservoir it is pumped back up to the top reservoir to begin the process again.

1.38 Now listen to a conversation and complete the notes.

Go over the notes with the class and ask the students to listen and complete them.

Play the listening passage and have the students complete the notes.

Answers

1 every day
2 five days a week
3 10.30 am
4 4.30 pm
5 two hours
6 power station
7 £4.50
8 £70.00

1.38 7 Listen again and circle three letters A–F.

Explain to the students that this is another kind of multiple-choice question – selecting from a list of alternatives – that they may be given in the test.

Go over the multiple-choice questions with the students.

Play the listening passage again and have the students choose the correct answers.

Answers

B D F

Language study: information questions

8 Study the examples and explanations.

Go over the examples and explanations with the students.

If you wish, play the passage again for students to listen to the examples in context again.

Explain that information questions have the same word order as statements, but that the students should be careful with yes/no questions. For example, *What time does the tour start?* becomes *Do you know what time the tours starts?* not *Do you know what time does the tour start?* You may also find a tendency for the students to over-rely on information questions using *I want to know ...* . Although this is not incorrect, it may sound a little impolite to some people.

Point out that the students need to be careful with *Would you mind ...?* A positive answer to these questions is *No, (I don't mind)* and a negative answer is *Yes, (I do mind)*.

Now decide which information question above is the most/least polite.

Answers

Starting with the most polite:
I wonder if you could give me some information
Would you mind telling me the group rate?
Could you tell me what Dinorwig is?
Can you tell me what the tour includes?

> **Additional activity: pronouncing information questions**
>
> Say the information questions as a model for the students.
>
> Have them listen to you and practise, paying attention to stress and intonation, especially to the falling intonation at the end of the question.

9 Work in pairs. Student A, ask for information and complete the notes. Student B, turn to assignment 6.1 and answer the questions.

Divide the class into Students A and B.

Refer Student A to the notes and ask them to write information questions for Student B to answer.

Refer Student B to assignment 6.1 and ask them to read the information and prepare to answer Student A's questions.

Put the students in pairs, remind them to use information questions and have them do the activity.

> **Background reading**
>
> The Eden Project aims to educate people about the relationship between 'plants, people and resources' and how to achieve a sustainable future. It is situated in Cornwall in the southwest of England and its centerpiece is three biomes, huge transparent dome structures housing plants and conditions that replicate the world's climates.

Reading

Go over the IELTS tasks with the students and make sure they understand what they will practise in this section.

1 **Work in pairs. Look at the picture and try to answer the questions.**

Direct the students to the picture and go over the questions with them. Questions 2, 3 and 4 are open for discussion. Question 4 practises prediction skills. Tell the students that more than one answer may be possible and that they should try to give as many of their own ideas as possible.

Put the students in pairs and have them answer the questions.

Answers

1 a hydroelectric power station. 2 C 3 A
4 open answers

Achieve IELTS: predicting

By predicting the content of a passage – reading or listening – the students give themselves a better chance of understanding the passage. They begin to use the resources from the passage, like the title, headings or any diagrams and pictures included. Moreover, they have already begun to engage with the passage and this will help them to understand the theme and topic more quickly because they are bringing their knowledge of the world to the passage.

Before reading or listening to a passage the students should ask themselves ...

- What is the main point of the passage?
- Where are the topic sentences in each paragraph?
- Which sentences give supporting information, like examples, definitions, and subsidiary points, and which give essential information?

Now read the passage and check your answers to question 4.

Ask the students to read the passage and check their answers to question 4.

Open answers

2 **Read the passage again. Do the statements agree with the information given in the reading passage?**

Go over the 'true', 'false' and 'not given' statements with the students.

Ask them to read the passage again and decide which statements are true, false or not given.

Answers

1 True – '24 per cent of the world's electricity' (line 3)

2 Not given

3 False – 'the energy that is generated from water depends not only on the volume but also on the difference in height between the dam and the water outflow' (lines 18–21)

4 True – 'some early hydroelectric systems used the flow of water over an existing waterfall, with no dam needed' (lines 25–26)

5 False – 'This requires two reservoirs: an upper reservoir where water is stored to provide power; and a lower reservoir where water enters from the upper reservoir after being used for power generation' (lines 64–70)

3 **Find words in the passage which mean ...**

Go over the definitions with the students and ask them to read the passage again and find the words.

Answers

1 generator 2 dam 3 reservoir 4 turbine
5 transformer

Now read the passage again. Label the diagram using the words in B.

Ask the students to read the passage again and label the diagram with the words in box B.

Answers

1 dam 2 reservoir 3 head 4 intake
5 penstock 6 turbine 7 outflow
8 transformer 9 generator

Language study: present passive

4 **Study the examples and explanations.**

Go over the examples and explanations with the students.

Explain that we use the present passive to talk about processes that take place in the present or are generally true.

We use the passive to put the important information at the beginning of the sentence or when the agent of the action (the person who initiates the action or event) is not known, not important or obvious (we do not need to mention them as everyone knows who they or are).

When we want to specify the agent, we usually add this at the end of the passive structure with by. However, there are a number of other phrases we use to do this.

Now look at the diagram and complete the passage with the verbs in brackets.

Direct the students to the diagram and have them read the passage.

Ask them to complete the passage with the correct form of the verbs in brackets.

Note that not all of these are passive.

Answers

1 are used   2 are put   3 are supplied
4 moves   5 is formed   6 is collected

➤ **Further practice:** *Achieve IELTS Workbook,* Unit 6 Language study

5 **Work in pairs. Student A, turn to assignment 6.2. Describe the diagram to Student B. Student B, label the diagram.**

Divide the class into Students A and B.

Refer Student A to assignment 6.2 and ask them to describe the diagram to Student B. Student B should label the diagram.

Go round the class and monitor for the correct use of the passive.

Answers

1 A wave chamber is set into the sea.
2 Water is pushed into the chamber.

3 Air is pushed and pulled by the waves.
4 A turbine is driven by the air.

➤ **Further practice:** *Achieve IELTS Workbook,* Unit 6 Reading

Now work in pairs and write a short paragraph about wave power.

Ask students to write a short paragraph about wave power. If you wish, you could have them do this in pairs. Students will practise writing about a process in detail in the writing section, so a short paragraph is all that is necessary at this point.

Suggested answer

A wave chamber is set into the sea. Water is pushed into the chamber by the movement of the sea. Air is pushed and pulled inside the chamber by the waves. The movement of the air drives a turbine inside the chamber. Electricity is generated by the turbine.

Writing

Go over the IELTS tasks with the students and make sure they understand what they will practise in this section.

1 **Work in pairs. Look at the picture and answer the questions.**

Direct the students to the picture.

Put the students in pairs and have them discuss the questions.

Open answers

2 **Look at the diagram. Complete the description with the words in C.**

Tell the students that a possible writing task is to describe a process.

If you wish, before they complete the description, you could ask the students to read the passage and decide how many stages of the process there are.

Ask the students to complete the description with the words in box C.
1 are moved/are turned
2 are turned/are moved
3 are connected
4 is generated
5 is increased
6 is sent
7 is taken

Now label the diagram. Use the words in D.

Go over the words with the students and explain that they are all parts of windpower energy production. Remind them that they have come across most of these in the reading passage.

Have the students label the diagram with the words.

Answers

1 blade   2 hub   3 shaft   4 gearbox   5 nacelle

Language study: sequence and purpose

3 **Study the examples and explanation.**

Go over the examples and explanations with the students.

Explain that we use phrases for sequence to help the reader (or listener) understand the order of information or event or a process. We use phrases of purpose to show why something is done.

Try to encourage the students to use these when if they have the task of describing a process.

Now work in pairs. Put the words and phrases in E into groups.

Refer the students to the words and phrases in E.

Tell the students to group them into words and phrases for purpose or for sequencing.

Answers

sequence: after that, next, secondly, the last thing, when, to begin with

purpose: in order to, so as to, so that

4 **Read the passage and answer the questions.**

Go over the questions with the students.

Ask them to read the passage and answer the questions.

Answers

1 organic matter   2 70–90%   3 four

Now read the passage again and find words which mean ...

Go over the definitions with the students.

Ask the students to read the passage again and find the words for the definitions.

Answers

1 combustion   2 pyrolysis   3 digestion
4 fermentation

5 **Look at the diagram and order the sentences.**

Go over the sentences with the students.

Ask them to look at the diagram and put the sentences in order.

Answers

1 E   2 C   3 B   4 D   5 A   6 F   7 G

Now write about the diagram using words and phrases for sequencing and purpose and passive sentences.

Ask the students to use the sentences in activity 6, and the words and phrases for sequencing and purpose in activity 4, to write a short text about the diagram. Tell them that in some cases they will need to write some passive sentences in the active form – they should not simply copy the sentences and join them with a word or phrase.

See page 62 for suggested answer and commentary.

> **Additional activity: describing a process**
> If you wish, you could ask the students to write a short paragraph about a process they are familiar with.

➤ **Further practice:** *Achieve IELTS Workbook,* Unit 6 Writing

Listening

Go over the IELTS tasks with the students and make sure they understand what they will practise in this section.

1 **Look at the picture and answer the questions.**

Direct the students to the picture.

Go over the questions with the class and have the students discuss them.

At the end of the discussion, get the answers from one or two pairs.

Answers

1 Australia, but could be in any other appropriate country.

2 The dishes collect energy from the sun to use in people's homes. (A more technical

answer is not necessary, however the picture shows concentrating collectors, as opposed to flat plate collectors, which focus the energy on a small area to produce a higher temperature than flat plate collectors.)

3 Open answers.

1.39 2 **Listen to a talk and match the names with the jobs.**

Tell the students that they will hear a talk about the Centre for Sustainable Energy.

Go over the jobs and explain any new words. Play the listening passage and have the students match the names with the jobs.

Answers

1 c   2 a   3 b   4 d

➤ **Further practice:** *Achieve IELTS Workbook,* Unit 2 Vocabulary activity 3

1.39 **Now listen again. Complete the notes and diagram.**

Play the listening passage again and have the students complete the notes and diagram.

You may wish to separate this activity into two distinct activities: firstly listening and completing the notes, secondly listening again and completing the diagram.

Answers

Notes: 1 Engineering   2 in 1980   3 30   4 about US$2 million   5 facilities

Diagram: 1 administration   2 (research) laboratories   3 research assistants' offices   4 seminar room   5 lecture room   6 Professor Karl Micova's office

3 **Work in pairs. Answer the questions.**

Go over the questions with the class and have the students discuss them.

At the end of the discussion, get the answers from one or two pairs.

Open answers

4 **Read the quiz and choose the answers.**

Go over the quiz with the students. Ask them to do the quiz. If you wish, you could ask them to do this in pairs, or compare their answers when they have finished.

The students will be able to check their answers in the next activity

1.40 **Now listen to a lecture and check your answers.**

Play the listening passage and have the students circle the correct letters.

Answers

1 C   2 B   3 C   4 B

1.40 5 **Listen again and label the diagram.**

Go over the diagram with the students and ask them to listen and label it.

Play the listening passage again and have the students label the diagram.

Answers

1 nuclear
2 energy
3 1,400
4 the atmosphere
5 plate
6 82
7 pump
8 tank

Now work in pairs and discuss the questions.

Open answers

➤ **Further practice:** *Achieve IELTS Workbook,* Unit 6 Listening

Speaking

Go over the IELTS tasks with the students and make sure they understand what they will practise in this section.

1 **Work in pairs. Decide which energy sources are sustainable.**

Go over the words with the students and explain that they are all sources or types of energy.

Have the students decide which energy sources are sustainable or renewable and which are not.

Answers

sustainable: hydroelectric ✓   solar ✓
nuclear ✓   geothermal ✓   wave ✓   wind ✓
non-sustainable: coal ✓   gas ✓   oil ✓

➤ **Further practice:** *Achieve IELTS Workbook,* Unit 6 Vocabulary activity 2; Unit 6 Pronunciation

2 Read the text and tick the things you do.

Go over the passage with the students and explain any unknown words, for example LCD stands for *liquid crystal display* (a low power display used for showing numbers on digital clocks, watches, etc.)

Ask the students to read the passage and tick the things they do.

If you wish, you could ask the students to do the activity in pairs, or compare their answers at the end of the activity.

Open answers

Now work in pairs. Compare your answers.

3 Read the topic and make notes.

Go over the notes with the students. If you wish, you could ask them to underline the important words and phrases.

Have the students make notes about the topics.

Now tick the rounding-off questions for the topic.

Go over the rounding-off questions with the students and ask them to decide which are appropriate questions to end part two of the test.

Answers

✓ Does your country have any solar power stations?

✓ How do you encourage other people to save energy?

✓ How does your country generate electricity?

✗ How many national parks are in your country?

Background reading

Explain to the students that rounding-off questions are used by the examiner to end part 2 of the test (the individual long turn), and move on to part 3 (the discussion). They take the candidate from the specific topic in the individual long turn and widen the topic into a freer discussion with the examiner.

---

4 Work in pairs. Ask each other about the topic and the relevant rounding-off questions.

Put the students in pairs and have them do the activity.

Open answers

➤ **Further practice:** *Achieve IELTS Workbook*, Unit 6 Study skills

Suggested answer

Firstly, waste is moved to a shredder, after which the waste is taken to a storage pit where it is mixed with organic waste. **Following this**, the waste is transported into the pyrolysis oven. **After that**, the oven is heated, without air, to about $450\,^\circ\text{C}$ in order to produce pyrolysis gas and other solid materials. At the next stage, the gas and solid materials are separated. **Next**, the hot gas is fed into a combustion unit. The gas is then taken to a generator so as to produce heat and gas.

Student's answer

The flow chart shows the process of producing energy from biomass. In the first stage, waste is moved to shredder. The shredder cut all the wastes into very small pieces. The second step, the shredded waste is taken to a storage pit. It is stored or mixed with organic waste. The third step is transporting the mixture into pyrolysis ovens. Then the mixture is heated without air, in the ovens at a high temperature which is about 450 C. Then the waste should be separated by gas and solid materials. After that the solid waste was produced. The waste in the separation is further subdivided into hot gas which is fed into a combustion unit. Next the waste is transported into generator. Some times later the heat and gas will be provided. The other way is after the process of separation, other solid materials was produced, such as solid waste. The way of dealing with solid waste is that it is taken to a waste site.

> **Comment**
> This writing presents an overview followed by an accurate description of the process. Good use is made of sequencing expressions, and vocabulary in general is adequate for the task. Errors in use of prepositions, articles and tense are noticeable, but the meaning is generally clear. This essay is likely to score a band 6.0.

Themes cities, megacities, districts, suburbs

Passages an article on megacities (reading); a conversation about a city, a lecture about suburbanisation (listening)

Language study comparative and superlative adjectives (introduction)

Express yourself talking about cities (introduction)

Achieve IELTS comparing graphs (writing)

Vocabulary

parts of a city *inner city, dormitory town, suburb, city centre*

adjectives for cities *overcrowded, quiet, inland, pleasant, new, dirty, large, small, noisy, spacious, dynamic, boring, clean, horrible, old, coastal, beautiful, cold, pleasant, humid, bad*

Background reading

The themes of talking about your home town and where you live often come up in the test.

This unit focuses on urban living and the processes of urbanisation, in particular the spread of the suburbs and the rise of megacities: cities with a population of over 10 million people. Students learn more about Sydney – the largest city in the world in terms of area, and about London and some of its districts.

Cosmopolitan

1 **Work in pairs. Ask each other the questions.**

Go over the questions with the class and have the students discuss them in pairs.

At the end of the discussion, get the answers from one or two pairs.

Open answers

2 **Match the opposite words.**

Go over the words with the students and explain any new words.

Ask the students to find the opposites.

Answers

overcrowded	spacious
quiet	noisy
inland	coastal
pleasant	horrible
new	old
dirty	clean
large	small
dynamic	boring

➤ **Further practice:** *Achieve IELTS Workbook,* Unit 7 Vocabulary

---

Additional activity: guess the city

If you wish, you could describe a town or city in your country using some of the adjectives and ask the students to guess which town or city you are talking about.

Now work in pairs. Describe your home town/city.

Put the students in pairs and have them describe their home town.

Open answers

 3 **Listen to a conversation and tick the words in 2 you hear.**

Tell the students they will hear a conversation about a city.

Play the listening passage and have the students tick the words in activity 2 they hear.

Answers

overcrowded ✓   quiet ✓   noisy ✓   spacious ✓
dynamic ✓   boring ✓   old ✓   coastal ✓

1.41 Now listen again and complete notes A. Write no more than three words and/or a number for each answer.

Go over the notes with the students and ask them to listen and complete each space with no more than three words or a number.

Play the listening passage again and have the students complete the notes.

Answers
1 Honshu island/north-east coast/Tokyo bay
2 15th century
3 12 million
4 2,000 km^2
5 13

Express yourself: talking about cities

1.42 Listen and complete the sentences.

Tell the students that they can use these words and phrases to give and ask for more information about a city.

Play the recording and have the students complete the sentences.

Answers
1 whereabouts   2 suppose   3 thought   4 Isn't

1.42 Now listen again and practise.

Play the recording again and have the students practise, paying attention to stress and intonation.

Language study: comparatives

4 **Study the examples and explanations.**

Go over the examples and explanations with the students.

If you wish, play the listening passage in activity 3 again for students to listen to the examples.

Explain that we use comparative adjectives to compare two or more things. Go over the rules for the formation of comparative adjectives, but you may want to explain that the rule for adjectives with more than two syllables is not as simple as it first appears. With most two-syllable adjectives we can use *more* + adjective + *than*. With a few two-syllable adjectives we can use *more* + adjective + *than* or adjective +*er*. Some of these are *lovely, quiet, simple, clever*.

Now work in pairs. Decide how to form the comparative adjectives of the words in B.

Ask the students to work in pairs and make comparative adjectives.

Answers
1 more beautiful than   2 colder than
3 more pleasant than   4 more humid than
5 worse than

> **Further practice:** *Achieve IELTS Workbook,* Unit 7 Pronunciation

5 **Write three sentences comparing your home town with Sydney or Tokyo.**

Refer the students to the charts in activities 3 and 6.

Ask the students to write at least three sentences comparing their home town with London or Tokyo or another city they are familiar with, paying attention to correct use of comparative adjectives.

If you wish, you could put the students in pairs and ask them to compare their answers.

Open answers

6 **Work in pairs. Discuss these questions.**

Direct the students to the pictures. Explain that they will complete the information about Sydney in the next activity.

Go over the questions with the class and have the students discuss them.

At the end of the discussion, get the answers from one or two pairs.

Open answers

Now read the passage and complete the chart for Sydney.

Ask the students to read the passage and complete the chart for Sydney.

Answers
location: south-east of Australia
founded: 200 years ago
population: 3.7 million
area (m2): 5,000 km2
number of universities: 5

7 **Answer the questions.**

Go over the questions with the class and have the students answer them. If you wish, you could ask the students to do the activity in pairs.

At the end of the activity, get the answers from one or two students.

Answers
1 Sydney harbour, the shoreline, the national parks
2 They are known for their love of sport
3 It can take half a day to travel across the city.
4 Open answers

Language study: superlatives

8 Study the examples and explanations.

Go over the examples and explanations with the students.

Explain that we use superlative adjectives to compare more than two things. Go over the rules with the students. Again, the rules for two-syllable adjectives can be slightly confusing, with some words taking the *-est* superlative form or *the most* + adjective. Some of these are *lovely, quiet, simple, clever.*

Common adjectives that are irregular in both comparative and superlative forms are *good, bad* and *far.*

Now answer the questions about London, Tokyo and Sydney.

Refer the students to the charts in activities 3 and 6.

Go over the questions with the class and have the students answer them.

At the end of the activity, get the answers from one or two students.

Answers

1 London (founded 50 AD)
2 Tokyo (12 million people)
3 Tokyo (13 universities)
4 Sydney (300 kilometres)

➤ **Further practice:** *Achieve IELTS Workbook,* Unit 7 Language study

9 Work in pairs. Compare three cities in your country

Put the students in pairs and have them do the activity.

At the end of the discussion, get the answers from one or two pairs.

Open answers

Speaking

Go over the IELTS tasks with the students and make sure they understand what they will practise in this section.

1 Label the pictures with these cities.

Direct the students to the pictures and have them match the cities with the pictures.

Answers

A Rio de Janeiro   B Singapore   C Istanbul
D Edinburgh   E Bangkok

 Now listen to a talk and decide which city the speaker talks about.

Play the listening passage and ask the students to decide which city is described.

Answer

Istanbul

 2 Listen again and number the subjects in the order you hear them.

Play the listening passage again and have the students put the things the speaker talks about in order.

Tell the students that this is one possible way of organising a description of a city.

Answers

1 location   2 geography   3 history
4 description   5 opinion

Pronunciation

 3 Listen and notice how the voice rises and falls.

Play the recording and have the students notice the rising intonation before and and the falling intonation on the last word of the list.

Answers

Europe and Asia

the Bosphorous on one side

and the Black sea on the other

founded by the Greeks and developed by the Romans

 Now listen again and practise.

Play the recording again and have the students practise, paying attention to stress and intonation.

4 Work in pairs. Student A, turn to assignment 7.1 and describe the city. Student B, decide which city Student A describes.

Direct the students back to the pictures in activity 1 and explain that Student A will describe one of these and Student B should try to guess which city it is.

Explain to the students that this activity is exam practise for part 2.

Split the class into Students A and Students B. Put the students into pairs and ask Student A to describe the city using the information in assignment 7.1 and any other information they can add (as long as it is not misleading).

Ask Student A to cover assignment 7.2.

Answer

Singapore

Now Student B, turn to assignment 7.2 and describe the city. Student A, decide which city Student B describes.

Ask Student B to turn to assignment 7.2 and describe the city for Student A to guess.

Answer

Edinburgh

5 **Read the topic and make notes.**

Go over the notes with the students. If you wish, you could ask them to underline the important words and phrases.

Have the students make notes about the topics.

Now tick the rounding-off questions for the topic.

Go over the rounding-off questions with the students and ask them to tick the questions the examiner may ask them.

Note: the examiner would not ask the candidate the second question as it makes the assumption that the student has been to Paris.

Answers

✓ How long have you lived there?

✗ Is it as nice as Paris

✓ Have you got any special memories about it?

✓ What other cities would you like to visit?

6 **Work in pairs. Student A, you are the examiner; interview Student B. Student B, you are the candidate; answer the questions.**

Have one student take the role of the examiner and the other student take the part of the candidate.

Put the students into pairs and ask them to do the activity.

If you wish, when the students have finished, ask them to swap roles and talk about the topic again.

Reading

Go over the IELTS tasks with the students and make sure they understand what they will practise in this section.

1 **Label the diagram. Use the words in C.**

Direct the students to the diagram and ask them to label it with the words in C.

Answers

A suburb   B inner city   C city centre
D dormitory town

Now work in pairs. Say where you live.

Ask the students to say which part of their town or city they live in and to add some more information about it.

Open answers

2 **Read the passage and choose the most suitable headings for sections A–E from the list of headings.**

Go over the list of headings with the students.

Ask them to read the passage and match the headings with the paragraphs.

Answers

1 A iii – 'defined as an urban area of more than 10 million inhabitants' (lines 2–3)

2 B ii – 'Megacities are the end result of the process of urbanisation' (line 5)

3 C vii – 'this movement away from cities does not mean that the city is dying' (line 11)

4 D vi – 'today the greater number are in developing countries' (lines 18–19)

5 E v – 'Megacities have a number of similar specific problems' (line 25)

Additional activity: active questioning

Write the title of the passage on the board and ask the students what they already know about megacities.

Then ask the students what they would like to know about megacities and write their questions on the board.

Give them five minutes to read the passage and check whether what they know is correct and whether any of their questions are answered.

Now read sections B and C again and complete the table. Use no more than three words.

Go over the table with the students,

Ask the students to read sections B and C again and complete the table with no more than three words.

Answers

1 moved into suburbs   2 moved into villages
3 the city spreads   4 areas merge together

3 Read the passage again. Do the statements reflect the claims of the writer?

Go over the 'true', 'false' and 'not given' statements with the students.

Ask them to read the passage again and decide which statements are true, false or not given.

Answers

1 False – 'low-level urban developments' (line 12)
2 Not given – The passage does not mention poorer people moving in, only richer people moving out.
3 True – 'From the old city develops a metropolitan area' (line 12)
4 False – 'today the greater number are in developing countries' (lines 18–19)
5 True – 'city problems are thought to be cause mostly by weak and unrepresentative city government' (lines 26–27)

4 Work in pairs. Discuss the questions.

Go over the questions with the class and have the students discuss them.

At the end of the discussion, get the answers from one or two pairs.

Open answers

➤ **Further practice:** *Achieve IELTS Workbook,* Unit 7 Reading

Listening

Go over the IELTS tasks with the students and make sure they understand what they will practise in this section.

1 Match the places in D with the pictures.

Direct the students to the pictures and ask them which city the photos are of.

Have the students match the words with the pictures.

Answers

A Houses of Parliament   B Hyde Park
C the British Museum   D Kensington Market   E Globe Theatre

2.3 2 Listen to a conversation and label map B with the places in 1.

Tell the students they will listen to a conversation and should label the map with the places in activity 1 as they listen.

Direct the students to map B and point out features such as the River Thames and Hyde Park.

Play the listening passage and have the students label the map.

Answers

1 Houses of Parliament   2 British Museum
5 Globe Theatre   6 Kensington Market
7 Hyde Park

2.3 3 Listen again and complete the notes with no more than two words for each space.

Go over the notes with the students and ask them to listen and complete them with no more than two words.

Play the listening passage again and have the students complete the notes.

Answers

1 government buildings   2 arts   3 musical
4 financial/business   5 north   6 wealthy

4 Work in pairs. Discuss which places in London you would like to visit and why.

Put the students in pairs and have them discuss where they would like to visit in London.

At the end of the discussion, get the answers from one or two pairs.

Open answers

5 **Read the notes and decide whether each answer is a number or other information.**

Explain to the students that an important part of preparing to listen is predicting what kind of information they will listen to.

Ask the students to read the notes and decide what kind of information they can expect in the answer.

Open answers

Now work in pairs. Discuss the possible answers.

Put the students in pairs and have them discuss their answers.

Open answers

 6 **Listen to a lecture and complete the notes in 5. Write no more than three words and/or a number for each answer.**

Play the listening passage and have the students complete the notes.

Answers
1 19th and 20th
2 40%
3 public transport
4 the cities
5 200 years
6 high-rise apartments

7 half a million
8 traffic congestion
9 private transport
10 overweight population

7 **Complete the chart with Southeast Asia (SA) or America/Australia (A/A).**

Go over the chart with the students and ask them to complete it.

If necessary, play the listening passage again and have the students complete the table.

Answers
1 SA   2 A/A   3 SA   4 A/A   5 SA

Now work in pairs. Discuss the questions.

Go over the questions with the class and have the students discuss them. Remind the students that suburbs in Australia tend to be made up of low-rise buildings with gardens, but in South Korea they tend to be made up of high-rise apartment blocks.

At the end of the discussion, get the answers from one or two pairs.

Open answers

➤ **Further practice:** *Achieve IELTS Workbook,* Unit 7 Listening

Writing

Go over the IELTS tasks with the students and make sure they understand what they will practise in this section.

1 **Work in pairs. Ask each other the questions.**

Go over the questions with the students.
Put the students into pairs and have them discuss the questions.

Open answers

Now look at the chart and answer the questions.

Go over the chart and the questions with the students.

Ask them to answer the questions.

Answers
1 the growth of cities from 1950–2015
2 Possible answers: northern and southern cities, new and old cities, developing and developed nation cities, growing and shrinking cities

3 Open answers

4 Open answers

2 Put the sentences into two groups.

Go over the sentences with the students and ask them to put the sentences into groups.

Answers

comparing/contrasting: 1, 3, 4, 5

classifying: 2, 6

Now underline the words and phrases for comparing, contrasting and classifying.

Ask the students to read the sentences in activity 2 again and underline the words and phrases for comparing, contrasting and classifying.

Answers

comparing/contrasting: 'In comparison with', 'When we compare', 'they have similar', 'on the other hand', 'In contrast with'

classifying: 'We can divide the cities into two main groups', 'We can also make a distinction between'

Achieve IELTS: comparing graphs

If the students are given a graph in the writing test, explain that it is very important that they describe it fully and do not include irrelevant information. The second thing they should do is try and group the information. The third thing they should do is compare the information they have grouped using appropriate phrases for classifying, comparing and contrasting. Candidates who do this score better in the test.

3 Underline the key words in the essay title and make notes.

Ask the students to read the title, underline the key words and make notes.

Suggested answer

The chart shows <u>the rate of growth</u> of eight cities in <u>developing</u> and <u>industrialised</u> countries between <u>1950</u> and <u>2015</u>. Write a <u>report</u> for a university lecturer <u>describing the information</u> in the chart.

Now write a 150 word report.

Ask the students to write a report about the chart.

Refer the students back to the language studies on comparatives and superlatives.

If you wish, you could ask them to include the sentences in activity 2, or just the words and phrases for classifying, comparing and contrasting.

See page 70 for suggested answer and commentary.

➤ **Further practice:** *Achieve IELTS Workbook,* Unit 7 Writing; Unit 7 Study skills

Suggested answer

The line graph shows the growth of cities between 1950 and 2015. On the vertical axis we can see the population of cities in millions and on the horizontal axis we can see the time in years.

From the information in the chart, we can divide the cities into two main groups. In the first group we can put cities like London and Paris where the population is growing very slowly or declining, for example, the population of London fell from around eight million in 1950 to seven million in 2005. In contrast, in the second group we can include cities such as Dhaka and Mumbai. In Dhaka the population rose very rapidly from thousands of people in 1950 to over 25 million people in 2005, and Mumbai where the population was about two million in 1950 and increased rapidly to approximately 22 million people in just 55 years.

We can also make a distinction between cities in developed and developing nations. In contrast with cities in developing nations like Dhaka and Mumbai, city populations in industrialised countries are growing at a much slower rate. New York's population grew at a slower rate, in Paris it levelled off at nine million, and in London it dropped.

In conclusion, we can see that the populations of the cities in many developed nation's cities have been overtaken by cities in developing nations.

Student's answer

From this chart we can see the rate of growth of population in different country between 1950–2015. We can make a distinction between cities in developed and developing nations.

The developed nations like New York in USA and some Europe cities the populations of these cities is growing steadily or declining. In contrast with cities like New York these developing nations like Dhaka and Mumbai where the population is growing very rapidly.

We can also devide the cities into other three main groups: cities from Asia, America and Europe. There are three cities from Asia, they are Tokyo, Mumbai and Dhaka. The arrange of the population of these cities generally very large and growing very fast. Compair with the city like Tokyo, cities in America where the population is growing steadily and the population in European nations are growing very slowly or declining.

The causation of the different rate of growth in different cities is the different history and culture in different nations.

> **Comment**
>
> This essay begins well with a good overview, but the information is not supported by data. Structures tend to be repetitive, and more complex sentences lose accuracy. This would be unlikely to score more than band 5.0.

Themes *mobile phones, digital devices*

Passages an article about how mobile phones work (reading); a lecture on the effect of mobile phones on human health (listening)

Language study real conditionals (introduction), *unless, in case* (reading)

Express yourself disbelief (introduction)

Achieve IELTS cue words (listening), timing and length (writing)

Vocabulary

mobile phone handsets *SIM card, hash key, star key, keypad, receiver, screen, charger, menu, battery*

deceptions *a scam, a rip off, to overcharge*

mobile communication networks *handset, base station, cell, frequency, cable*

digital devices *MP3 player, palmtop, digital recorder, mobile phone, flash drive*

other *to bar someone/something, a voucher, a prize, concern, evidence, issue, precaution, risk*

Background reading

The theme of this unit is mobile communication. One of the first things international students do when they reach university is buy a mobile phone. This unit looks at mobile phone bills and some deceptive practises the student needs to be aware of. It gives the student practise in dealing with automated answering systems and explains how mobile phones work. The unit goes on to look at developments in technology more generally and introduces part 2 of the writing test – the discursive essay.

In touch

Background reading

In touch means *to be in contact with someone*, hence the phrases: *I'll be in touch, keep in touch, be in touch with you later.*

---

1 **Work in pairs. Discuss the questions.**

Direct the students to the opening picture and ask them what the relationship is between the unit title and the picture.

Ask the students how many of them have a mobile phone and how often they use it.

Go over the questions with the class and have the students discuss them.

At the end of the discussion, get the answers from one or two pairs.

Open answers

2 **Work in pairs. Look at picture A and discuss what has happened.**

Direct the students to picture A and ask them to work in pairs and discuss what has happened.

If you wish, you could ask the students what they think the people say.

Open answers

2.5 Now listen to a conversation and check your answers.

Play the listening passage for general understanding and have the students check their answer.

Answer

Sara, the young woman, has received an extremely large mobile phone bill and has dropped her cup because of the shock.

Background reading

Companies like these do operate in the UK, although they do not charge as much as £20 per minute, they can charge up to £15 per minute. Recently, the UK government has been trying to stop such practices.

2.5 3 Listen again and complete the bill.

Go over the bill with the students and ask them to listen for detail and complete it.

Play the listening passage again and have the students complete the bill.

Answers

1 £164.50   2 line rental   3 15   4 £15.30
5 07887 683 702   6 £50.00

Now circle the correct letter A–C.

Go over the multiple-choice questions with the students and ask them to choose the correct answers.

If you wish, you could play the listening passage again and for the students to check their answers.

Answers

1 C   2 B   3 A

> **Additional activity: bills**
>
> If you wish, you could ask the students who has received a large bill they did not expect, what they said when they saw it and what happened later.

Express yourself: disbelief

Tick the expressions of disbelief.

Go over the expressions from the listening passage with the students and tell them that two of the expressions do not express disbelief.

Ask the students to tick the expressions of disbelief.

Answers

I don't believe it. ✓   that can't be right. ✓
No way! ✓   there must be a mistake ✓
that can't be right ✓

Note: we use *What's up?* to ask what is happening and *Never mind* to say something does not matter.

Now listen and practise.

Play the recording and have the students practise the expressions paying attention to stress and intonation.

4 **Work in pairs. Choose a situation and write a conversation.**

Go over the situations with the students.

Put the students into pairs and have them write a short conversation about the situation they chose.

Now practise the conversation.

Ask the students to practise their conversation. When they have finished practising, ask one or two pairs to act out their conversation for the class.

Open answers

5 **Label the picture. Use the words in A.**

Direct the students to the picture.

Go over the words with the students and explain that they are all parts of a mobile phone.

Have the students match the words in box A with the pictures.

Answers

1 receiver   2 menu   3 screen   4 charger
5 battery   6 SIM card   7 hash key   8 star key
9 keypad

Note: *SIM card* stands for Subscriber Identification Module or Subscriber Identity Module card.

6 **Listen to a message and write the key next to the options.**

Go over the keys with the students and ask them to listen for detail and match the key with the options.

Play the listening passage and have the students match the numbers and options.

Answers

A to return to the menu = *
B to join from another network = 5
C other enquiries = 3, 6
D information about premium line charges = 4
E to upgrade your phone = 2
F to talk to someone = 3
G information about your recent order = 1
H join the network = 2
I more information about the advertisements = 1
J to hear the options again = #

Language study: real conditionals

7 **Study the examples and explanations.**

Go over the examples and explanations with the students.

If you wish, play the passage again for students to listen to the examples in context.

Explain that we use the real conditionals to talk about the result of an action (if the action happens). We use real conditionals for general or scientific truths, or to talk about the certain result of an action – in this case the result of pressing a telephone key pad button will result in a message.

We can replace *if* with *when* or *as soon as* when we are more certain that something will happen: *When you press that button the bomb will explode.*

Now write an answerphone message for your school or another organisation.

If you wish, you could put the students in pairs for this activity.

Make sure the students use real conditionals in their automated answer messages.

At the end of the activity, get one or two automated answer messages from the students.

Open answers

➤ **Further practice:** *Achieve IELTS Workbook*, Unit 8 Language study activity 1; Unit 8 Pronunciation

8 **Work in pairs. Ask each other these questions.**

Go over the questions and example with the class and have the students discuss them.

At the end of the discussion, get the answers from one or two pairs.

Open answers

➤ **Further practice:** *Achieve IELTS Workbook*, Unit 8 Vocabulary

Reading

Go over the IELTS tasks with the students and make sure they understand what they will practise in this section.

1 **Match the words in B with the definitions.**

Go over the words with the students and explain that they are all from the reading passage later in the activity.

Have the students match the words and definitions.

Answers

1 to bar someone or something
2 a scam
3 a prize

4 a voucher
5 to overcharge
6 a rip-off (note: verb – to rip someone off)

Now read the passage and find two scams and three ways to avoid them.

Refer the students to the reading passage and have them find two scams and three ways to avoid them.

Answers

Scams:
1 You call a number back at a very high call rate and someone keeps you talking.
2 You call to collect a prize, but get a voucher worth much less than the cost of the call.

Avoiding scams:
1 When you get an unwanted call, ask the network to bar the number.
2 When there is a short time to claim your prize, think twice about calling.
3 Do not ring a missed call unless you already know the number.

Language study: *unless, in case*

2 **Study the examples and explanation.**

Go over the examples and explanations with the students.

If you wish, play the passage again for students to listen to the examples.

Explain that we use *unless* to mean that if you do not do something, a particular (undesirable) action or event will follow: *Unless you hurry up, we'll be late.*

We use *in case* to talk about something we should do in advance in order to avoid something happening.

Now complete the conversation. Use *unless*, *if*, *in case* or *when*.

Go over the conversation with the students and ask them to complete it.

Tell the students they will check their answers in the next activity.

2.8 3 **Listen to the conversation and check your answers.**

Play the listening passage and have the students check their answers.

Answers

1 If 2 if 3 unless 4 when/if 5 when
6 in case

Now work in pairs. Practise the conversation.

Have the students work in pairs and practise the conversation.

If you wish, you could ask one or two pairs to act out their conversation for the class.

➤ **Further practice:** *Achieve IELTS Workbook,* Unit 8 Language study activity 2

4 **Work in pairs. Circle the correct letter A or B.**

Go over the questions with the class and have the students discuss them.

At the end of the discussion, get the answers from one or two pairs.

Answers

1 B   2 B (Nokia)   3 B

Background reading

In the US, mobile phones are more commonly called *cell* (or *cellular*) phones. While the percentage of people using mobile phones in the US is above 50%, in Europe (and Asia) the percentage is much nearer 90%.

Nokia's market share of the mobile phone market in 2004 was 29.2%, nearly twice the amount of its nearest competitor Motorola.

It is illegal to drive a vehicle while using a mobile phone in the UK, even if the traffic is not moving.

---

5 **Label the diagram. Use the words in C.**

Go over the words with the students and explain that they are all parts of a mobile phone network.

Have the students match the words with the definitions.

Answers

1 handset   2 cell   3 cable   4 frequency

6 **Read the passage and order pictures A–C.**

Direct the students to the pictures.

If you wish you could ask the students how they think a mobile network works, i.e. ask them to predict the content of the passage.

Ask the students to read the passage for general understanding and order pictures A–C.

Answers

1C   2B   3A

Now label the pictures.

Ask the students to label the pictures with words from the reading passage.

Answers

1 base station   2 control channel
3 duplex channel   4 registration request
5 switching centre

7 **Read the passage again. Complete the sentences with *handset, base station* or *switching centre*.**

Ask the students to read the passage again and complete the sentences.

Answers

1 base stations   2 Switching centres
3 switching centres   4 handset   5 base station

8 **Work in pairs. Ask each other the questions.**

Go over the questions with the class and have the students discuss them.

At the end of the discussion, get the answers from one or two pairs.

Note: the final question prepares the students for the listening section, so you may wish to make a note of their answers for use later.

Open answers

➤ **Further practice:** *Achieve IELTS Workbook,* Unit 8 Reading

Speaking

Go over the IELTS tasks with the students and make sure they understand what they will practise in this section.

1 **Label the pictures with the words in D.**

Direct the students to the pictures and ask them to name as many of the pictures as they can.

Have the students match the words in box D with the pictures.

Answers

1 MP3 player   2 palmtop   3 digital recorder
4 mobile phone   5 flash drive

Now work in pairs. Talk about an item or piece of equipment you would like to have.

If you wish, you could elicit more electronic devices that the students would like to have.

Put the students in pairs and ask them do the activity. Make sure they give reasons for their answers.

Open answers

2 Read the topic below and make notes.

Go over the topic with the students. If you wish, you could ask them to underline the important words and phrases.

Have the students make notes about the topic.

Open answers

2.9 Now listen to a talk and decide what items in activity 1 are described.

Play the listening passage and have the students tick the items in activity 1 the speakers talk about.

Answers

digital recorder ✓   MP3 player ✓

2.9 3 Listen again and complete the table.

Go over the table with the students and ask them to listen for detail and complete it.

Explain the word *aluminium* before the students do the listening activity.

Play the listening passage again and have the students complete the table.

Answers

	1	2
size/weight	small, light	9 cm, light
material	aluminium	metal and plastic
colour	–	pink
other features	length of recording time (also: buttons, battery in the back, tough)	holds up to 1,000 songs

Pronunciation

4 Read the phrases and mark the stressed words.

Go over the phrases with the students.
Play the recording and have the students underline the stressed words.

Answers

this is <u>very</u> handy
the <u>best</u> thing about it is
I carry this <u>everywhere</u> with me
I <u>definitely</u> couldn't live <u>without</u> it

2.10 Now listen and practise.

Play the recording again and have the students practise the expressions, paying attention to stress and intonation.

5 Work in pairs. Discuss the topic in 2.

Put the students into pairs and ask them to do the activity.

Have one student take the role of the examiner and the other student take the role of the candidate.

If you wish, when the students have finished, ask them to swap roles and talk about the topic again.

Open answers

6 Read the topic and example questions below. Underline the key words.

Explain to the students that this activity practises part 3 of the speaking test, the discussion.

Go over the topic with the students and ask them to underline the key words.

Suggested answers

Let's consider the <u>usefulness</u> of <u>electronic items</u>.
1 <u>Which</u> electronic items are <u>popular</u> in your country?
2 Do <u>new</u> electronic items make our <u>lives more complicated</u> or <u>more convenient</u>?

Now make notes for your answer.

Have the students make notes about the topic. Explain that they will not have the opportunity to make notes on the topic in the test, but this is to help them in the next activity.

Open answers

7 Work in groups. Ask each other the questions and discuss the topic.

Put the students into small groups and have them discuss the questions.

Although the students will not use group work in the test, at this point they may find it confidence building to work in small groups.

However, if you wish, you could put the students in pairs to do the activity, to reproduce test conditions.

Listening

Go over the IELTS tasks with the students and make sure they understand what they will practise in this section.

There is one listening passage, a lecture, which is split into two parts.

1 **Match the words with the definitions.**

Go over the words with the students and explain that they are all from the listening passage.

Have the students match the words with the definitions.

Answers

1 c 2 e 3 d 4 a 5 b

2 **Read the title of the lecture and decide what things will be included.**

This activity practises predicting the content of a listening passage.

Refer the students to the title in activity 3 and have them think about what the lecture will include. Note: the notes below the title will help the students guess the subjects in part 1 of the lecture, but not part 2.

Get the answers from the class and write them on the board for the students to check against the listening passage.

2.11/12 **Now listen to the lecture and check your answers.**

Play the whole listening passage – parts 1 and 2 – and have the students check their answers.

Open answers

2.11 3 **Listen again. Complete the notes for the first part of the lecture only. Write no more than three words or a number for each answer.**

Go over the notes with the students and ask them to listen and complete them with no more than three words or a number.

Play part 1 of the listening passage again and have the students complete the notes.

Answers

1 essential part   2 possible health effects
3 transmitters/antennas   4 remember things
5 safe/not dangerous

Now answer the questions.

Go over the questions with the students and ask them to answer them from memory.

If you wish, you could play part 1 again.

1 £300   2 1920s   3 the government

Achieve IELTS: cue words

In the notes for listening passages, the words immediately before the gaps are cues that can help attentive students to get the answers. The

students need to know that the word before the gap may be repeated in the listening passage, or that a synonym for the word may be used. In either case, by underlining the cue words and phrases before the gap, they will have a better chance of getting the answer. As soon as the students hear the words or phrase immediately preceding the gap (the cue for the answer), they should be ready to write the answer.

Now read the notes in part 1 again and compare the cue words with the recording script.

Refer the student to CD2 track 11 for part 1 of the lecture and ask them to compare the cue words with the recording script.

Answers

Cue words and phrases	Listening passage
they **think** their mobile **phone** is an	– **considered** their **phone** to be **an** essential part

Note: after *an* the answer must begin with a vowel.

This lecture is **about** the	– I'm going to **look at**
The main **concerns** are **about**	– **concerns** about mobile phones **centre around**
radio waves **said** they **couldn't**	– they **claimed** they **weren't able to**
enough knowledge to say mobile phones are	– do not **have** enough **knowledge**

> **Additional activity: recollecting**
>
> Before the class goes on to listen again to part 2 in detail, ask the students what they can remember about it from the first listening and write it on the board for the students to check against the listening passage.

2.12 4 **Listen again. Complete the notes for the second part of the lecture. Write no more than three words and/or a number for each space.**

Go over the notes with the students and ask them to listen and complete them with no more than three words or a number.

Play part 2 again and have the students complete the notes.

Answers

1 the skin   2 tiredness   3 2.5   4 power lines
5 remember and learn   6 brain cancer
7 the 1980s

Answers

Cue words and phrases	Listening passage
Mobile phones **heat up**	– mobile phones can **heat up**
people **complain of**	– they often **complain of**
mobile phone users are	– **mobile phone users are**
there is **a link between**	– **a relationship between**
ability to concentrate	– **ability to concentrate**
the **connection** between mobile phone use and	– the **link** between mobile phone use and
people who have used mobiles **since**	– people who have used mobiles **from**

Now work in pairs. The lecture gives contrasting reasons for 1–4 – what are these?

Go over the example with the students and see if they can remember the contrasting information about the effects of mobile phone use.

You may wish to refer the students back to CD2 track 12 to do this.

Answers

1 mobile phones heat up the skin; they are not powerful enough to damage us
2 people complained of tiredness; not the same under laboratory conditions
3 users are 2.5 times more likely to develop cancer; researchers say there is no direct link to mobile phones
4 there is a relationship between childhood cancer and power lines; it is a different kind of radiation

5 **Work in pairs. Student A, make a list of advantages of using mobile phones. Student B, make a list of disadvantages of using mobile phones. Try to give examples to support your points.**

Ask the students to make a list of either advantages or disadvantages of using mobile phones. If you wish you could put the students into groups to do this.

Now discuss the advantages and disadvantages of mobile phones.

Put the students in pairs and ask them to discuss the advantages and disadvantages of mobile phones.

Open answers

➤ **Further practice:** *Achieve IELTS Workbook*, Unit 8 Listening

Writing

Go over the IELTS tasks with the students and make sure they understand what they will practise in this section.

1 **Do the quiz.**

Go over the quiz with the students and ask them to answer the questions.

Open answers

Now turn to assignment 8.1 and read your results

Ask the students to look at the key in assignment 8.1 and see if they agree with it.

Open answers

2 **Read the writing task below and decide if the statements are true or false.**

Go over the writing task and explain to the students that this is the format for the essay title in part 2 of the writing test.

Ask the students to read the title and decide if the statements are true or false.

Answers

1 False – 40 minutes
2 False – no specialist knowledge, i.e. some general knowledge
3 True
4 False – 250 words

3 **Order the stages of writing an essay from the first thing to the last.**

Go over the stages with the class and ask the students to put them in order.

Tell the students that there may be more than one possible answer and they should try to give reasons for their decisions on the order.

Suggested answers

1 Read the title and underline the key words.
2 Make a list of ideas: decide which are relevant and reject irrelevant ideas.
3 Break your ideas into sections and make a plan.
4 Write the essay.
5 Read the essay for sense.
6 Read the essay again for mistakes and correct the mistakes.

Now decide how many minutes to spend on each stage.

Remind the students that they only have 40 minutes to complete the essay.

Ask the students to say how much time they will spend on each stage. Try to encourage them to stay within a 10-minute limit for preparation and proof reading.

Achieve IELTS: timing and length

Timing is critical in any test or exam. Running out of time leads to underlength essays and essays that are really a set of notes or bullet point. The latter will lead to the student losing points due to poor paragraphing. Although taking a watch into the test will help, it is by practising before the test and improving writing speed that the student will really help themselves. Ask the students to keep a note of how many words they are able to write within a time limit and record how their writing speed improves with practice.

4 **Read the title of the writing task in activity 2 again and underline the key words.**

Refer the students back to the writing task in task 2 and ask them to underline the important words and phrases.

Suggested answer

You should spend about <u>40 minutes</u> on this task. Present a written argument or case to an educated reader with no specialist knowledge of the following topic.

<u>Advances</u> in <u>mobile communication technology</u> have been one the most <u>important developments</u> in the late twentieth century. To what extent do you <u>agree</u> or <u>disagree</u> with this statement?

You should use your <u>own ideas, knowledge and experience</u> and support your arguments with <u>examples</u> and <u>relevant evidence</u>. You should write at least <u>250 words</u>.

5 **Read the list of ideas. Decide which are relevant (R), which are irrelevant (I) and which are partially relevant (PR).**

Go over the ideas with the students and ask them to decide which are relevant to the essay title in activity 2, which are not relevant, and which are partially relevant.

Answers
1 Relevant
2 Relevant
3 Not relevant
4 Relevant
5 Not relevant
6 Not relevant/partially relevant
7 Partially relevant

Now work in pairs. Think of examples and ideas to support the relevant points.

Ask the students to think of examples and ideas to support the relevant (and, if you wish, partially relevant) points.

Open answers

6 **Work in pairs. Read the writing task below and ...**

Go over the writing task and make sure the students understand the title.

It is a good idea to go through the process of examining an essay title, brainstorming ideas and organising ideas as a class for the first few writing test essay titles.

Ask the students to read the title and underline the key words. Then ask them to make a list of ideas, explain that they should write as many ideas as possible. If you wish, you could ask the students to do this in small groups or pairs. When they have finished, get some ideas from the class and put them on the board. As a class decide which ideas are relevant which are not relevant. Finally, ask the students to group their ideas into sections, or paragraphs, and have them come up with supporting points and examples. Next, the students should decide on the order of the sections (or paragraphs).

Explain to the students that they will practise writing full essays from Unit 11. However, if you wish, you could ask them to write the essay from the notes they have prepared.

Suggested answer to 1

<u>Mobile phones</u> have many <u>benefits</u>, but the <u>effects</u> of mobile phones on <u>human health</u> mean the <u>dangers</u> are <u>greater</u> than the <u>benefits</u>. To what <u>extent</u> do you <u>agree</u> or <u>disagree</u> with this statement?

▶ **Further practice:** *Achieve IELTS Workbook*, Unit 8 Writing; Unit 8 Study skills

Themes university blues, health and fitness, sports, lifestyle

Passages an article on how to keep fit (reading); instructions for yoga, a tour of a sports centre (listening)

Language study *should (n't) / must (n't)* (listening), modal verbs for possibility and certainty (reading)

Express yourself talking about ability (introduction)

Achieve IELTS descriptions (speaking)

Vocabulary

sports *rugby, kendo, yoga, rowing, windsurfing, fencing, lacrosse, handball, cricket, surfing, American football, football, basketball*

parts of the body *hips, spine, back, elbow, bottom, shoulders, stomach, head, chest, arm, neck, leg*

actions *spread, stretch, bend, breathe (in/out), raise, lift*

gym equipment *leg curl bench, pec deck, stair climber, rowing machine, treadmill*

fitness *muscular strength, cardiovascular, muscular endurance, flexibility, motor co-ordination*

Background reading

Sports are a very important part of student university life. Traditionally, Wednesday afternoons were kept free for students to do sport activities, and some universities still have Wednesday afternoons free in the UK. Most universities have their own sports centres and facilities, and a wide range of sports societies for students to join. Universities also compete with each other nationally, and internationally in the World University Championships and the World University Games.

Students who achieve excellence at a particular sport and represent their university at it earn a blue. A blue, in sport, is a person chosen to represent his

or her university. The term originated at Oxford and Cambridge Universities, Oxford wearing dark blue and Cambridge light blue jackets, caps and scarves. A 'full' blue is awarded for those sports which are regarded as senior, for example athletics, soccer, cricket, rowing and rugby football. Half-blues are awarded for minor sports, for example squash and lacrosse. Some sports originally given half-blue status later secured full blues, for example hockey.

Get fit!

1 **Label the picture. Choose from the words in A.**

Go over the words with the students and explain that they are all sports

Have the students decide which sport is in the picture.

Answer

rowing

Additional activity: guess the sport

If you wish, you could ask the students which other sports they know and write them on the board.

If you know the class well, you could have a student come to the front of the class and mime one of the sports while the other students try to guess which one it is.

Now work in pairs. Say which sports you have tried.

Ask the students to discuss which sports they have tried.

Put the students in pairs and have them discuss the topic.

At the end of the discussion, get the answers from one or two pairs.

Open answers

2.13 2 **Listen to the conversation and tick the sports you hear.**

Play the listening passage and have the students tick the sports they hear.

Answers

rugby ✓   kendo ✓   yoga ✓   rowing ✓
windsurfing ✓   basketball ✓

2.13 **Now listen again. Complete the sentences with no more than three words or a number for each space.**

Go over the notes with the students and ask them to listen and complete each space with no more than three words or a number.

Play the listening passage again and have the students complete the notes.

Answers

1 level 5   2 on weight   3 go and do   4 Japan
5 free course   6 loose clothing   7 286

3 **Answer the questions.**

Go over the questions with the students.

If you wish, play the listening passage again and have the students choose the correct answers.

Answers

1 The wind blew him to the other side of the lake and he had to walk back without shoes.
2 He says rugby players are big, strong and aggressive.
3 You score points by hitting your opponent's body with a sword.

Express yourself: talking about ability

2.14 **Listen and practise the expressions.**

Play the recording and have the students practise the expressions, paying attention to stress and intonation.

Now match the two parts of the sentences.

Go over the beginnings and ends of the sentences with the students and explain that they are all ways of talking about ability.

Ask the students to pay attention to the prepositions and have them match the beginnings and ends of the sentences. We use good at + activity; good with + equipment; good in/on + water, air, land.

Answers

1 b   2 c   3 a

4 **Work in pairs. Ask each other these questions.**

Go over the questions with the class and have the students discuss them.

At the end of the discussion, get the answers from one or two pairs.

Open answers

➤ **Further practice:** *Achieve IELTS Workbook,* Unit 9 Vocabulary

5 **Work in pairs. Read the title of the passage below and discuss what a *blue* is.**

Go over the title with the students and ask them to work in pairs and discuss what a blue is. Explain to them that they do not need to come up with a correct answer, at this point they should try to come up with as many ideas as possible before reading the passage.

Answer

A blue is an award given at university for students who are good at sports.

Now read the passage and answer the questions.

Go over the questions with the students and ask them to read the passage, answer the questions and check their answers to the previous activity.

Answers

1 handball   2 business   3 Yes, Denmark
4 seven days a week   5 win a medal in the Olympics

2.15 6 **Listen to an interview and circle A–D.**

Go over the multiple-choice questions with the students.

Explain any new words, for example *tadpole* (a frog after it emerges from the egg, and before becoming a recognisable frog).

Play the listening passage and have the students choose the correct answers.

Answers

1 C   2 C   3 B   4 A

2.15 **Now listen again and complete the sentences with no more than three words.**

Go over the notes with the students and ask them to listen and complete each space with no more than three words.

Play the listening passage again and have the students complete the notes.

Answers

1 represent their university   2 full   3 half
4 blue jacket   5 blue scarf   6 blue cap

7 Work in pairs. Discuss the questions.

Go over the questions with the class and have the students discuss them.

At the end of the discussion, get the answers from one or two pairs.

Open answers

Listening

Go over the IELTS tasks with the students and make sure they understand what they will practise in this section.

1 Label the picture. Use the words in B.

Go over the words with the students and explain that they are all parts of the body.

Have the students match the words with the pictures.

Answers

1 neck   2 shoulder   3 spine   4 back   5 elbow
6 hips   7 chest   8 hand   9 arm   10 bottom
11 stomach   12 leg

Now match the words in C with the definitions.

Go over the words with the students and explain that they are all actions associated with different parts of the body.

Have the students match the words with the definitions.

```
Additional activity: question and answer

If you wish, you may like to have students
ask you about words for other parts of the
body they wish to know (within reason).
```

Answers

1 bend   2 spread   3 stretch   4 raise   5 lift
6 breathe (in/out)

2.16 2 Listen to a yoga instructor and complete the notes with no more than three words for each answer.

Go over the notes with the students and ask them to listen and complete each space with no more than three words.

Play the listening passage and have the students complete the notes.

Answers

1 spine   2 bottom   3 raise   4 shoulders
5 spread   6 hips   7 spine   8 lower back
9 shoulders   10 muscles

3 Work in pairs. Ask each other the questions.

Go over the questions with the class and have the students discuss them.

At the end of the discussion, get the answers from one or two pairs.

Open answers

2.17 4 Listen to a tour of the sports facilities. Label the plan below with the words in D.

Go over the words with the students and explain that they are all types of exercise machine.

Direct the students to the plan.

Play the listening passage and have the students label the plan.

Answers

1 treadmill   2 cycling machines
3 rowing machine   4 cable cross machine
5 pec deck   6 chin up bar

2.17 Now listen again and match the machines with the parts of the body.

Go over the words with the students and ask them to listen for detail and match the machines with the parts of the body.

Play the listening passage again and have the students match the machines with the parts of the body.

Answers

1 e   2 d   3 b   4 c   5 a

➤ **Further practice:** *Achieve IELTS Workbook*, Unit 9 Listening; Unit 9 Vocabulary

Language study: *should(n't)*, *must(n't))*

Go over the examples and explanations with the students.

If you wish, play the passage again for students to listen to the examples.

Explain that we use *should* to give suggestions and advice whereas for strong advice and obligation we use *must*.

Now complete the sentences with *must*, *mustn't*, *should* or *shouldn't*.

Answers

1 should   2 must   3 should   4 should

➤ **Further practice:** *Achieve IELTS Workbook*, Unit 9 Vocabulary activity 2

Pronunciation

2.18 **6**   **Listen and notice the pronunciation of *should(n't)*.**

Play the recording and ask the students to listen and notice the pronunciation of should(n't). Tell the students to pay particular attention to the end of the word as in the negative it is pronounced /ʃʌdn/ rather than /ʃʌdnt/.

2.18   **Now listen again and practise.**

Play the recording again and have the students practise the sentences.

➤ **Further practice:** *Achieve IELTS Workbook*, , Unit 9 Pronunciation

7   **Complete the sentences.**

Go over the beginnings of the sentences with the students and do the first one as an example.

Ask the students to complete the sentences.

Now work in pairs. Compare your answers.

Put the students into pairs and have them compare and discuss their answers.

At the end of the activity, get one or two answers from some of the pairs.

Open answers

➤ **Further practice:** *Achieve IELTS Workbook*, Unit 9 Language study

Reading

Go over the IELTS tasks with the students and make sure they understand what they will practise in this section.

1   **Label the pictures with the words in E.**

Go over the words with the students and have them match the pictures with the words in E.

Answers

1 cycling   2 weights   3 jogging   4 juggling
5 t'ai chi

2   **Work in pairs. Decide which statements are true and which are false.**

Go over the statements with the students and have them decide which are true.

Tell them that they will check their answers in the next part of the activity.

At the end of the discussion, get the answers from one or two pairs.

Now read the passage and check your answers.

Ask the students to read the passage quickly and check their answers.

Answers

1 False – 'experts recommend covering five key areas of physical fitness' (line 6)
2 True – 'physical exercise as a long-term lifestyle choice, as opposed to a quick fix' (lines 17–18)
3 False – 'Little and often is better than one big session' (line 23)
4 True – 'Experts recommend walking 10,000 steps a day' (lines 29)

3   **Choose the best title for the passage.**

Go over the titles with the students and explain *holistic* (to do with the whole person, not just physical aspects of a person), *crash-diet* (a diet in which is done intensely over a short period of time), and *posture* (the way a person holds themselves).

Ask the students to choose the best title for the reading passage.

Answer

ii The holistic approach to fitness

4   **Read the passage again. Do the statements reflect the claims of the writer?**

Go over the 'yes', 'no' and 'not given' statements with the students.

Ask them to read the passage again and decide which statements reflect the claims of the writer.

Answers

1 Not given
2 Yes – 'They could be more prone to injury' (lines 12–13)
3 No – 'achieving a good level … can be easier than people think' (line 16)
4 Yes – 'easiest way to adopt a balanced routine is to become more active in your day-to-day tasks' (lines 27–28)

Now complete the summary. Choose one or two words from the reading passage for each answer.

Go over the summary with the students and have them complete each space with one or two words from the reading passage.

Answers

1 (personal) fitness   2 holistic attitude
3 often   4 balanced routine   5 tasks

➤ **Further practice:** *Achieve IELTS Workbook,* Unit 9 Reading

Language study: possibility and certainty

5 **Study the examples and explanations.**

Go over the examples and explanations with the students.

Explain that we use *can, could, may* and *might* to talk about possible outcomes of actions, *is* and *will* to talk about an outcome we are certain will happen as a result of certain actions. In addition to these verbs, we can use *likely to be, probably* and *possibly* to talk about possible outcomes.

Ask the students to give you one or two more examples using these structures.

Now complete the sentences.

Go over the beginnings of the sentences with the class and ask the students to complete them with their own ideas, paying attention to verbs for possibility and certainty.

If you wish, you could ask the students to do the activity in pairs, or compare their answers at the end of the activity.

Open answers

6 **Work in pairs. Discuss an activity or sport you do or want to try.**

Put the students in pairs and have them discuss the topic.

At the end of the discussion, get the answers from one or two pairs.

Open answers

➤ **Further practice:** *Achieve IELTS Workbook,* Unit 9 Language study activities 4, 5 and 6

Speaking

Go over the IELTS tasks with the students and make sure they understand what they will practise in this section.

1 **Work in pairs. Decide which equipment is used in the sports in F.**

Go over the words with the students and explain that they are all types of sports.

Direct the students to the picture of the sports equipment and have them match the pictures with the words in F.

Answers

A American football   B cricket   C football
E surfing

2.19 **Now listen to four descriptions and put the sports in F in the order you hear them.**

Tell the students they will listen to four descriptions and that they should number the sports in the order they hear them.

Play the listening passage and have the students number the sports.

Answers

1 surfing   2 football   3 American football
4 cricket

2.19 2 **Listen again and complete the sentences.**

Go over the sentences with the class and ask the students to listen for detail and complete the spaces.

Explain that the sentences contain phrases the students may find useful in the test.

Play the listening passage again and have the students complete the sentences.

Answers

1 is used, made of   2 a kind of, wear
3 a variety, positioned across   4 straight pieces of wood, to hit

Now label equipment A–D with the words in G.

Direct the students back to the pictures and ask them to label the pictures.

Answers

A helmet   B wicket   C shin pads   D leg rope

Achieve IELTS: descriptions

Tell the students that if they are asked to describe an object in the speaking test, or if they forget the name of an object, for example, an item of sports equipment, they should try to describe it rather than simply say, *I forgot*, or *I don't know how to say it.* This is not seen as a sign of poor English by the examiner, but as a strategy that helps the student communicate – the student will not lose marks and may even gain marks.

3 **Work in pairs. Student A, turn to assignment 9.1. Describe the object to Student B. Student B, decide which object Student A describes.**

Divide the class into Students A and B.

Refer Student A to assignment 9.1 and ask them to describe the object to Student B.

Student B should look at the pictures and guess which object Student A is describing.

If you wish, you could make the activity more challenging by asking Students B to close their books and guess.

Put the students in pairs and have them do the activity.

Answer

C a snorkel

> **Additional activity: 20 questions**
>
> Put the students in groups.
>
> Explain that one student will think of an item of sports equipment, but not tell the other students.
>
> The other students should try to guess the object by asking a series of questions, but must stop at 20 questions.
>
> If the other students cannot guess the item within 20 questions, the student has another go.

4 **Read the topic below and make notes.**

Go over the notes with the students. If you wish, you could ask them to underline the important words and phrases.

Have the students make notes about the topics.

Now work in pairs. Student A, you are the examiner; turn to assignment 9.2. Student B, you are the candidate. Follow Student A's instructions.

Put the students into pairs and ask them to do the activity.

Have one student take the role of the examiner and refer them to assignment 9.2 for their script. This is very close to what they will hear during the test.

If you wish, you could use assignment 9.2 for one of the students each time they are asked to do speaking test part 2 practise.

If you wish, when the students have finished, ask them to swap roles and talk about the topic again.

Writing

Go over the IELTS tasks with the students and make sure they understand what they will practise in this section.

1 **Look at the picture and answer the questions.**

Direct the students to the picture and have them discuss the questions.

Tell them they will be able to check their answers in the next part of the activity.

Now read the passage and check your answers.

Ask the students to read the passage and check their answers.

Answers

1 a pedometer
2 The pedometer is activated when your feet hit the floor. It then measures the total distance and calories burned.

2 **Work in pairs. Ask each other these questions.**

Go over the questions with the class and have the students discuss them.

At the end of the discussion, get the answers from one or two pairs.

Open answers

3 **Read the essay title below and underline the key words.**

Go over the title with the students and ask them to underline the key words.

Suggested answers

<u>Prevention is better than cure</u>. It is better to <u>spend money on preventing illnesses</u> by promoting <u>healthy living</u> rather than spending

it trying to make people better <u>after they are ill</u>.

To what extent do you <u>agree</u> or <u>disagree</u> with this statement?

4 **Work in pairs. Write your main points.**

Put the students in pairs and ask them to discuss and write their main points.

Now write an example for each point.

Have the students write one or two examples for each of their main points.

5 **Read paragraphs A–D in the reading passage. Compare them with your main points.**

Ask the students to read the passage quickly and compare their main points with those in the passage.

Open answers

6 **Read the paragraphs again and put them in the right order.**

Ask the students to read the passage again and order the paragraphs.

Answers

1 C 2 A 3 D 4 B

Now answer the questions.

Go over the questions with the class, then ask the students to read the passage and answer the questions.

Explain to the students that they will be tested on paragraphing. They should separate their main points into clear paragraphs, introduce their points and link between paragraphs. They should not use bullet points or dashes to introduce their points.

Answers

1 There is one point per paragraph.
2 The main point comes near the beginning of the paragraph.
3 I'm going to look at, I would like to argue that, I'm going to discuss, if we now look at

7 **Read the essay title and underline the key words.**

Go over the title with the students and ask them to underline the key words.

Suggested answer

Present a written argument or case for <u>an educated reader</u> with <u>no specialist knowledge</u> of the following topic.

<u>Modern life</u> is becoming more and more <u>stressful</u>, and many people now suffer from <u>stress-related illnesses</u>. What are <u>the causes</u> of this stress, and <u>what can be done</u> to overcome the problem?

Now work in pairs. Write your main points and decide on their order.

Put the students in pairs and ask them to discuss the order of their main points.

8 **Write about the topic. You should write at least 250 words.**

If you wish, you could set this for homework.

If you do this task in class, you could set a time limit of 40 minutes as test practise.

See page 86 for suggested answer and commentary.

➤ **Further practice:** *Achieve IELTS Workbook*, Unit 9 Writing

Suggested answer

These days life in general is faster, busier and more demanding than in the past. People are expected to work longer hours and achieve more in their careers. In this essay I will look at how this effects people's everyday lives and in particular, how this effects their health.

In my opinion there are two major factors that cause stress inside and outside work. Firstly I will look at pressure at work. Inside work, people are being asked to be more and more competitive. They have competition from inside their company – from people under them working for promotion; they have competition from other companies and in addition there is competition from companies in other countries. All of this leads to longer working hours, increased pressure and increased stress. If this is hard for men, it is twice as hard for women who work as they also have to look after a family.

Secondly, I will go on to demands outside work. Increasingly, better communication means that advertisers and other people are able to sell us things perhaps we cannot afford, do no need and do not really want. The problem is that when a product becomes fashionable, people's children would like to have one and this places more pressure on parents to buy these things so that even at home where people should be able to relax, there is still pressure and stress.

In my view, there are no easy solutions to this. People need to make time for themselves in their private life and to make sure that their working life does not take up valuable family time. Another way of helping with stress is to do regular exercise and eat well. However, in my opinion the main way of avoiding stress is to keep work at work and keep our own time separate.

Student's answer

Many people are now suffering from stress-related illnesses. However the causes of the stress are diverse. For example, the rate of the divorce is getting higher in the present time. But in those cases, people who might receive the stress are not the parents, but their children. If they are very sensitive, some could not eat, drink even get out from the room. In fact, some people are suffering from undernourishment because they can not take much energy into the body in case they stop eating from the stress. The stress-related illnesses damage their body as a result. Therefore the possible solution towards stress-related illnesses is to be confident and to see a counsellor.

As ordinary people seem not to have a specified knowledge about that kind of illness, the best thing to do is to have a proper medical examination. In addition to this, another best thing to do is to be confident. Once people have stress, it is supposed to be hard to recover and keep their mental normal as it was. This is because even though the person tries to be normal, its body does not respond immediately. Usually it takes long while that the body functions like before it stopped. If the body does not functions as expected, the motivation will go down again and be back to the same situation. Therefore the solution is to be confident making sure that everything goes well.

> **Comment**
> Most of the main points are relevant to the question, but some are unclear, especially towards the end of the essay. The writing is generally logically organised, with an attempt at paragraphing, and some complex sentences are attempted. This is likely to score a band 6.0.

Themes charities, student voluntary work

Passages charities and state organisations (reading); volunteering at university, charity in the USA and Europe (listening)

Language study giving more information (reading)

Express yourself asking for details (introduction)

Achieve IELTS giving definitions and examples (speaking)

Vocabulary

charities *sponsor, collection, fundraise, support (a cause), donate, volunteer*

political systems *conservative, GDP, income, labour, socialist, welfare*

Background reading

There is some disagreement about what the term RAG stands for, but many people say that it stands for *Raising and Giving*. Most universities in the UK have a RAG committee which organises fundraising events through the year. However, the main effort is made in RAG week, during which students take part in many different events for charities. The funds raised by students are distributed to different charities each year. Events include raids or collections, sponsored hitchhiking, abseiling, bungee jumping and so on.

Universities also contribute to society by directly placing students to work as volunteers with charities and other non-profit organisations. This is seen as a good way for students to improve their employment chances, as they are able to put their skills into practise and gain transferable skills such as team working.

RAG week

1 **Work in pairs. Look at the pictures and the leaflet. Discuss the connection between them.**

Direct the students to the pictures and refer them to the leaflet.

Ask the students to work in pairs and discuss the connection between the pictures and the leaflet.

At the end of the discussion, get the answers from one or two pairs.

Answer

The pictures show some of the events in the leaflet.

Now look at the pictures and decide which events they show

Ask the students to decide which events from the leaflet they can see.

Answers

A RAG parade   B sponsored hitch
C sponsored abseil

2 **Read the text and circle the correct letter A–C.**

Go over the multiple-choice question with the students and have them choose the correct answer.

Answer

C

Now answer the questions.

Go over the questions with the students. Then ask them to read the passage and answer the questions.

Answers

1 raising and giving
2 five types of event are mentioned in the text – collections, music events, parachute jumps, hitchhikes and trips – but we are not told how many of each
3 once a year

3 **Read the passage again and match the words in A with the definitions.**

Go over the words with the students and explain that they are all connected to charities.

Have the students read the passage again and match the words with the definitions.

Answers

1 sponsor   2 donate   3 fundraising
4 collection   5 support   6 volunteer

 **4** **Listen to a conversation and circle four letters A–F.**

Go over the multiple-choice question with the students.

Play the listening passage and have the students choose the correct answers.

Answers

A, C, D, F

They do not discuss a collection by the film society, but the film society joining the collection on Saturday, they do not mention the sponsored parachute jump.

5 **Listen again and answer the questions.**

Go over the questions with the students.

Play the listening passage again and have the students answer the questions.

Answers

1 He was not sure what it was so he did not say anything (he kept quiet).
2 The students are going to collect money in swimwear (trunks and bikinis) in winter at the coast.
3 People give a small amount of money for each hour it takes to get to the destination. The students must reach the destination by getting a free ride from motorists.

Express yourself: asking for details

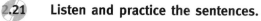 **Listen and practice the sentences.**

Go over the phrases with the students and explain that they are ways of asking for more information. Note: *What's the catch?* is a colloquial expression.

Play the recording and have the students practise the expressions, paying attention to stress and intonation.

Now work in pairs. Student A, look at assignment 10.1. Student B, ask for details about the fundraising event.

Refer the students to the poster then divide the class into Students A and B.

Refer Students A to assignment 10.1. Ask them to read the information and prepare to answer Student B's questions.

Put the students in pairs and have them do the activity.

Reading

Go over the IELTS tasks with the students and make sure they understand what they will practise in this section.

1 **Match the charities with their main purpose.**

Direct the students to the pictures and ask them what, if anything, they already know about the organisations. If you wish, you could ask them if they are surprised that all of these organisations are charities.

You may want to explain *beneficial* (having a good effect), *permanent* (lasting a very long time), *overcome* (solve), and conquer (beat).

Ask the students to read the main purposes and match them with the charities.

Answers

1 A   2 B   3 E   4 D   5 C

Now work in pairs. Discuss the questions.

Go over the questions with the class and have the students discuss them.

At the end of the discussion, get the answers from one or two pairs.

Open answers

2 **Read the passage and match the figures with the statements.**

Go over the statements and figures with the students.

Ask the students to read the passage quickly and match the statements with the figures.

If you wish, you could put a limit on the amount of time the students have to do this.

Answers

1 d   2 c   3 b   4 a   5 e

3 **Read the passage again. Do the statements reflect the claims of the writer?**

Go over the 'yes', 'no' and 'not given' statements with the students.

Ask them to read the passage again and decide which statements are reflect the claims of the writer.

Answers

1 Yes – 'the voluntary sector is now as competitive as big business, and as desperate to create brand loyalty as any supermarket giant' (lines 8–10)
2 No – 'The difference between the richest and poorest charities is not necessarily wrong' (lines 21–22)
3 No – 'The charities which have millions of pounds have a huge responsibility for providing services in the public sector' (lines 34–37)
4 Not given (the government, not business is giving more money)
5 Yes – 'In a way it is good … The concern is that …' (lines 64–71)

Now complete the summary. Choose one or two words from the reading passage for each space.

Go over the summary with the students. Then ask them to read the passage in activity 2 and answer the questions using no more than two words.

Answers

1 brand loyalty   2 huge differences   3 wrong
4 specific purpose   5 government
6 the independence

Language study: giving more information

4 **Study the examples and explanations.**

Go over the examples and explanations with the students.

Explain that we use relative clauses to give more information about a person (*who*), place (*where*), time (*when*), or thing (*which, that*).

A basic test of a defining relative clause is whether the subject of the sentence can be identified if the clause if left out. Compare:

The charities which have millions of pounds have a huge responsibility for providing services in the public sector …

and

The charities have a huge responsibility for providing services in the public sector…

In the first example, we are clearly considering only charities with a lot of money, in the second example it is not clear which charities we are referring to.

Equally, a good test of whether or not a relative clause is non-defining is to take it out. Compare:

460 organisations, which represent just 0.28 per cent of the entire sector, have an annual income of more than £10 million.

and

460 organisations have an annual income of more than £10 million.

In these examples, the sense of the sentence is not changed by missing out the relative clause.

Now complete the sentences. Use *who, when, which* or *that* with correct punctuation.

Go over the sentences with the students. Ask them to write out the sentences in full with an appropriate relative pronoun.

Remind the students that they need to pay attention to punctuation.

Answers

1 A volunteer is someone who does work without pay.
2 RAG is a student organisation which raises money for charity.
3 Robin, who lives in the room next to Tao, is a volunteer for Oxfam.
4 Community-based charities are charities which are set up for a specific purpose.
5 The RAG committee, which has eight members, has its meetings in the Union bar.

➤ **Further practice:** *Achieve IELTS Workbook,* Unit 10 Language study

5 **Work in pairs. Discuss the questions.**

Go over the questions with the class and have the students discuss them.

If you wish, you could refer the students back to the reading passage in activity 2.

Answers

1 The government; funding is increasing as more services are given to charities to operate.
2 It shows that the government trusts the charities; it may undermine the independence of charities.
3 People spent more on the National Lottery; because of damaging stories about the management of charities.

➤ **Further practice:** *Achieve IELTS Workbook,* Unit 10 Reading: Unit 10 Vocabulary

Speaking

1 **Work in pairs. Read the sayings, discuss what they mean and if you agree.**

Go over the saying and the quotation with the class and have the students discuss them.

At the end of the discussion, get the answers from one or two pairs.

Suggested answers

1 People need to be kind to the people they are closest to.
2 Charity is giving something up that you value.

2 **Read the topic and rounding-off questions and underline the key words.**

Go over the topic with the students and ask them to underline the key words.

Make sure the students also read the rounding-off questions.

Suggested answers

<u>Describe</u> a <u>charity</u> or a <u>good cause</u>.

You should say:

<u>what</u> the charity or good cause <u>does</u>

<u>how</u> it <u>helps</u> people

and <u>why</u> you find this charity or good cause particularly <u>interesting</u>

Have you ever <u>given</u> to a charity or <u>good cause</u>?

Would you <u>like to work</u> for a charity or good cause?

2.22/24 3 **Listen to three speakers and match the speakers with pictures A–C.**

Direct the students to the pictures.

Play the listening passage and have the students decide which charity the speakers are talking about.

Answers

speaker A – Oxfam   speaker B – the Big Issue
speaker C – the National Trust

Now work in pairs. Decide which speaker gives the best answer and why.

Put the students in pairs and ask them to decide which speaker gave the best answer and why.

Answer

Speaker 2 gives the best answer because the talk contains the most information.

2.23 4 **Listen to speaker 2 again. Does he ...**

Play speaker 2 again and have the students decide what the speaker includes in his talk.

Answers

introduce the topic ✓   give a definition ✓
give an explanation ✓   give an example ✓
give an opinion ✓

Achieve IELTS: giving definitions and examples

During part 2 of the speaking test, the students have the opportunity to give a longer example of their spoken ability. If the students can give examples from their personal experience and define terms or items unfamiliar to the examiner, this will help them give a fuller and more interesting long turn.

Pronunciation

5 **Decide which words are linked.**

Explain to the students that sounds are often linked together between words, for example:
The IELTS course.
In this case an additional /‿/ links the two vowels.
Ask the students to decide which words in the phrases are linked.

Answers

The‿organisation I'd like to talk about
Let me‿explain
so‿it gives them some respect

2.25 **Now listen and practise.**

Play the recording and have the students practise the phrases, paying attention to the linked sounds.

6 **Make notes about Part 2 (in task 2) and Part 3.**

Refer the students back to the topic in activity 2 and have them read the topic in activity 6.

Having practised parts 1, 2 and 3 separately, the students will be asked to practise the parts together from this unit onwards.

Now work in pairs. Ask each other about both topics.

Have one student take the role of the examiner and the other student take the role of the candidate.

Put the students into pairs and ask them to do the activity.

If you wish, when the students have finished, ask them to swap roles and talk about the topic again.

Listening

Go over the IELTS tasks with the students and make sure they understand what they will practise in this section.

There are two listening passages. The first is a talk which is split into two parts. The second is a lecture.

1 **Work in pairs. Discuss the advantages of doing volunteer work.**

Put the students in pairs and have them discuss the advantages of volunteer work.

Get two or three answers from the class and write them on the board so that they can check their ideas in activity 2.

Open answers

2 **Read the form and decide which projects you would like to do.**

Go over the form with the students and explain any new words, for example *helpline* (a telephone service for people who need help or sometimes just someone to talk with).

Ask the students to decide which project they would like to do. If you wish, at the end of the activity you could put the students in pairs or small groups to discuss their answers.

2.26 3 **Listen to a talk and check your answers to activity 1.**

Play the listening passage and have the students check their answers.

Explain that they are listening for general understanding this time and that they will hear the passage again in the next section and listen for greater detail.

2.26 4 **Listen to part 1 again and complete the notes. Write no more than three words for each answer.**

Go over the notes with the students and ask them to listen and complete each space with no more than three words.

Play the part 1 of the listening passage again and have the students complete the notes.

Answers

1 volunteer organisations/local community groups
2 state school
3 databases
4 marketing and fundraising
5 translating and interpreting

2.26 4 **Listen to part 2 again and choose three letters A–E.**

Go over the multiple-choice questions with the students.

Play the part 2 again and have the students choose the correct answers.

Answers

1 B, C, E
2 A, C, D (E is implied but it is not stated)

Now work in pairs and ask each other the questions.

Go over the questions with the class and have the students discuss them.

At the end of the discussion, get the answers from one or two pairs.

Open answers

6 **Work in pairs. Decide which statements are true (T) and which are false (F).**

Go over the statements with the students.

Ask them to work in pairs and decide which statements are true and which are false.

Tell them they will be able to check their answers in activity 8.

7 **Match the words in B with the definitions.**

Go over the words with the students and explain that they are all about politics and economics.

Have the students match the words with the definitions.

Answers

1 socialist   2 income   3 conservative   4 GDP
5 welfare   6 labour

2.27 8 **Listen to a lecture and complete the table.**

Go over the table with the students and ask them to listen for detail and complete it.

Play the listening passage and have the students complete the table.

Answers

1 60%   2 30%   3 24%   5 $57 ($141 in UK) 6 200 years ago

After you have played the listening passage, go back to activity 6 and have the students check their answers.

2.27 9 Listen again circle the correct letters A–C.

Go over the multiple-choice questions with the students.

Play the listening passage and have the students choose the correct answers.

Answers

1 B   2 A   3 C

10 Work in groups. Discuss the statements.

Put the students into groups of three and have them discuss the statements.

Open answers

> **Additional activity: a debate**
>
> If you wish, you could structure the group discussion as a formal debate.
>
> Put the students into groups of four and split the group into two teams: for and against.
>
> The debate is structured:
>
> Team 1, student 1 (for) introduces their point of view and presents one or two points from their argument.
>
> Team 2, student 1 (against) introduces their point of view and presents one or two points from their argument.
>
> Team 1, student 2 (for) presents one or two points from their argument and concludes.
>
> Team 1, student 2 (against) presents one or two points from their argument and concludes.

➤ **Further practice:** *Achieve IELTS Workbook,* Unit 10 Listening; Unit 10 Pronunciation

Writing

Go over the IELTS tasks with the students and make sure they understand what they will practise in this section. *Achieve IELTS* deals with introductions and conclusions after dealing with topic sentences and paragraphing. This is because introductions and conclusions are usually the last parts of an essay to be completed.

1 Work in pairs. Discuss the questions.

Go over the questions with the class and have the students discuss them.

At the end of the discussion, get the answers from one or two pairs.

Suggested answers

1 It is usually thought to be good practise to leave the introduction to an essay until the end.
2 Things to include are: some background to the topic, why the topic is important, an outline of the structure of the essay.

Now read the title below and underline the key words.

Go over the title with the students and ask them to underline the key words.

Suggested answer

Today's charities are taking over duties which are the responsibility of the government. Governments, not charities, are responsible for people's welfare. To what extent do you agree or disagree with this statement?

2 Read the introduction and decide if the sentences are true (T) or false (F).

Go over the statements with the students.

Ask them to read the introduction and decide which statements are true and which are false.

Answers

1 False   2 True (they are registered with the government)   3 True

Now complete the introduction with *where, which* or *who*.

Ask the students to read the introduction again and complete it with the relative pronouns.

Answers

1 which   2 who   3 who   4 where

3 Read the introduction again and order A–D.

Ask the students to read the introduction again and order A–D.

1 D 2 C 3 A 4 B

4 Work in pairs. Discuss the title below.

Go over the title with the students and underline the key words.

Ask the students to discuss their ideas in pairs. You may want them to make notes of any key points in preparation for the next part of the task.

Suggested answer

Although <u>giving help to people</u> who need it is thought to be a <u>good thing</u>, in fact many <u>people have stopped</u> giving <u>donations</u> to charities. Today, <u>people do not trust charities</u>.

Now decide what to include from your discussion in the essay.

Have the students decide what information to include in the essay from their discussion.

5 Write an introduction to the essay in activity 4. Use the framework.

Go over the words and expressions used in essay introductions with the students and have them write an introduction for the title in activity 4.

Suggested answer

Recently, many people were concerned that giving to charities was a waste of money. This was because of reports that the money we gave to charities was not reaching the people who needed the help, but was being used by the charitable organisation itself to pay its employees, officers and bills. One purpose of a charity however is to help people who need it, and so people felt that charities were not achieving their real aim. In this essay I will look at the causes of this and if people still do not trust charities or whether people have changed their minds.

6 Read the paragraph and decide if it is a summary, a conclusion or both.

Ask the students to read the conclusion to the essay title in activity 1.

Ask them to decide if it is a summary of the main points in the essay, a conclusion, or both a summary and a conclusion.

Answer

Both: it summarises the main points of the argument and then goes on to draw a conclusion.

Now find ...

Ask the students to read the conclusion again and find phrases for 1–3.

Answers

1 In my opinion, I also believe, I think that
2 I'd like to summarise my main points
3 In conclusion

7 Write a conclusion for the essay title in 4. Use the framework below.

Go over the framework with the students.

Ask the students to use the phrases in activity 6 to write a short summary or conclusion (or both) to the essay title in activity 4.

In order to do this more effectively, you may want to ask the students to plan two or three main points for the essay.

Suggested answer

To sum up my main points: although charities in the past may have had large and expensive organisations, nowadays many charities make sure that most of the money we give goes directly to the people who need it. In conclusion, I belief that although people might have lost some trust in charities in the past, charities have worked hard to build up people's trust in them again and that charities are better and more efficient at what they do today than they were in the past.

....
Additional activity: timed essay

Now that the students have the introduction and conclusion to the essay, you may want to ask them to complete the essay under timed test conditions.
....

➤ **Further practice:** *Achieve IELTS Workbook*, Unit 10 Writing; Unit 10 Study skills

UNIT 11
Work

Themes work, interviews, changes in patterns of work, careers and careers advice

Passages working at home (reading); careers advice service, employment tests (listening)

Language study talking about preferences (introduction), second conditional (reading section), opinions (writing)

Express yourself saying goodbye (introduction)

Achieve IELTS giving examples (writing)

Vocabulary

jobs *barista, waiting staff, shop assistant, kitchen hand, care worker, surgeon, personnel manager, software engineer, interpreter, lecturer*

reasoning *verbal reasoning, numerical reasoning, diagrammatical reasoning, abstract reasoning, aptitude*

work *absence, leave, attitude, anxiety, turnover, job-hunting, occupation, recruitment, training , vocation, salary, responsibility, teamwork, work environment, job satisfaction, job security, holidays, traditional industry, service industry, heavy industry*

Background reading

Many students in the UK and Australia take part-time jobs during university and college to finance their education, especially as they usually do not live at home and have the extra costs of rent, food, bills, going out and so on. International students can also work in the UK for up to 20 hours per week (but no more).

Recently, a whole new vocabulary has developed around coffee and coffee bars. The waiters are called *baristas*, a coffee with milk is a *latte*, a coffee with chocolate powder on top is a *cappuccino*, and a coffee mixed with chocolate is called a *mocha*.

Person wanted

1 **Name the job in the picture above. Choose from the words in A.**

Direct the students to the picture and ask one or two questions about it: 'Where do you think he is working? What does his job involve? What do we call a cup of a small amount of very strong coffee?' (an espresso).

Go over the words with the students and explain that they are all types of jobs.

Have the students choose the correct word for the picture.

Answer

Barista

Now match the job in the picture with the advertisement.

Go over the advertisements with the students and ask them to match the job in the picture with an advertisement.

Answer

Person needed for busy coffee bar.

2 **Work in pairs. Discuss the questions.**

Go over the questions with the class.

Put the students in pairs and have them discuss the questions.

At the end of the discussion, get the answers from one or two pairs.

Open answers

2.28 3 **Listen to the conversation and answer the questions.**

Go over the questions with the students.

Play the listening passage and have the students answer the questions.

Answers

1 He has spent his grant.
2 He has lectures in the morning.
3 He is worried about his social life in the evenings.
4 Care worker

2.28 **Now listen again and complete the job advertisements.**

Refer the students to the job advertisements and ask them to predict what could complete the advert, for example a place, an adjective, a date, a number, and so on.

Play the listening passage again and have the students complete the advertisements.

Answers

1 experience   2 shop   3 team   4 Saturday
5 040 931 602

4 **Read the advertisements again and find words that mean ...**

Ask the students to read the advertisements again and find the words for the definitions.

Answers

1 energetic   2 reliable   3 considerate
4 motivated   5 enthusiastic

Language study: preference

5 **Study the examples and explanation.**

Go over the examples and explanations with the students.

If you wish, play the passage again for students to listen to the examples.

Explain that we often use *prefer* with an *-ing* form (*I prefer working in the morning*). However, where we use a clause which introduces an alternative, we use *prefer* with *to* + infinitive, in the sense of *I prefer to work in the morning rather than in the evening*. In this example, *rather* (*than*) begins the clause which introduces the clause giving the alternative to working in the morning.

Now complete the sentences.

Go over the sentences with the students and have them complete each space with a phrase from the language study.

Answers

1 'd prefer   2 'd rather   3 wouldn't mind
4 wouldn't want

Pronunciation

2.29 **6** **Listen and mark the way the voice rises and falls in the sentences in 5.**

Play the recording and have the students mark the intonation in the sentences in 5.

Answers

I'd rather not work in the morning.

I wouldn't want to work at night.

I wouldn't mind working at the weekend.

I('d) prefer to work in the afternoon.

2.29 **Now listen again and practise.**

Play the recording again and have the students practise the expressions, paying attention to stress and intonation.

➤ **Further practice:** Achieve IELTS Workbook, Unit 11 Pronunciation

7 **Work in pairs. Discuss which job in 1 you would prefer and why.**

Put the students in pairs and have them discuss which jobs they would prefer, or would rather not do, and why.

Make sure the students attempt to use the phrases in activity 5.

Open answers

Now discuss the questions.

Go over the questions with the class and have the students discuss them.

At the end of the discussion, get the answers from one or two pairs.

Open answers

2.30 **8** **Listen to an interview and complete the application form.**

Go over the form with the students and ask them to listen and complete it.

Play the listening passage and have the students complete the form.

Answers

1 morning   2 gardening   3 student
4 surfing   5 immediately

> **Additional activity: the successful candidate**
>
> Ask the students to work in pairs and decide if they should give the student the job or not.
>
> At the end of the discussion, get the answers from one or two pairs.

Open answers

2.30 9 **Listen again and circle the correct answer A–C.**

Go over the multiple-choice questions with the students.

Play the listening passage again and have the students choose the correct answers.

Answers

1 C   2 A   3 C

Express yourself: saying goodbye

2.31 **Listen and complete the sentences.**

Play the recording and have the students complete the sentences.

Tell the students that the phrases are for formal situations like an interview or the IELTS test.

Answers

1 for coming, nice   2 journey   3 too, Hope

Now practise the sentences.

Have the students practice the sentences. If you wish, you may want to play the recording again.

10 **Work in groups of three. Choose a job from 1 and hold an interview for it.**

Put the students into groups of three and ask them to choose a job from task 1 to hold an interview for. If you wish, it could be a job of the students' own choice.

Students A and B should think of questions to ask Student C. If you wish, you could refer them back to the audioscript to get ideas for questions. However, it is better that the students adapt the activity to their location.

Meanwhile, Student C should prepare one or two questions for the interviewers.

Ask the students to conduct the interview.

> **Additional activity: letter of application**
>
> If you wish, in order to practise for the general writing module, you could have the students write a letter of application for one of the adverts. Then ask them to exchange letters and reply to each other's letter of application.

Reading

Go over the IELTS tasks with the students and make sure they understand what they will practise in this section.

1 **Work in pairs. Ask each other the questions.**

Go over the sentences with the class and have the students ask each other the questions.

At the end of the discussion, get the answers from one or two pairs.

Open answers

2 **Look at the picture and the title of the passage. Write three things you think the passage contains.**

Direct the students to the picture and refer them to the title.

Ask the students to predict three things that will be in the reading passage.

If you wish, you could write their predictions on the board for the students to refer to later.

Open answers

Now read the passage and check your answers.

Ask the students to read the passage quickly and check their predictions.

Open answers

3 **Match the words in B with the definitions.**

Go over the words with the students and explain that they are all about work and worries about work.

Have the students match the words with the definitions.

Answers

1 anxiety   2 turnover   3 attitude   4 absence
5 leave

4 **Read the passage again and choose four letters A–F.**

Go over the multiple-choice questions with the students and have them read the passage again and choose the correct answers.

Answers

A (lines 8–10)   B (lines 20–23)
E (lines 61–63)   F (lines 69–70)
Not C – it reduces costs to the health service.
Not D – this is not mentioned.

Now find words and phrases in the passage that mean ...

Go over the definitions with the students.

Ask the students to read the passage again and find the words for the definitions.

Answers

1 impact (line 10)
2 back up (line 26)
3 assessment (line 35)
4 flexible (lines 21, 57)
5 critical (line 56)

5 **Read the passage again. Do the statements agree with the information given in the Reading passage?**

Go over the statements with the students.

Ask them to read the passage again and decide which statements are true, false or not given.

Answers

1 True (lines 12–15)	2 Not given
3 True (line 41–42)	4 Not given
5 False (lines 63–66)	

6 **Work in pairs. Ask each other the questions.**

Go over the questions with the students.

Put the students in pairs and have them discuss the questions.

At the end of the discussion, get the answers from one or two pairs.

Open answers

Language study: second conditional

7 **Study the examples and explanation.**

Go over the examples and explanations with the students.

If you wish, play the passage again for students to listen to the examples.

Explain that we use the second conditional to talk about actions, situations and events that we can imagine happening if certain conditions are fulfilled. In contrast with real conditionals, with the second conditional these conditions are less likely to happen. For example, *If they did not do the job, someone else would do it ...* – it is not very probable in this case that the person will leave the job.

You may wish to point out that we typically use the second conditional to give advise to other people: *If I was John, I'd ...* , and the irregular use of *were* in *If I were you, I'd ...* .

Now complete the sentences using the words in brackets.

1 had, would work   2 Would, leave, was
3 didn't have, would apply   4 would be, had
5 wouldn't do, paid

➤ **Further practice:** *Achieve IELTS Workbook,* Unit 11 Language study

8 **Work in pairs. Ask each other the questions.**

Go over the questions with the class and have the students discuss them.

Encourage them to use second conditional structures.

At the end of the discussion, get the answers from one or two pairs.

Open answers

➤ **Further practice:** *Achieve IELTS Workbook,* Unit 11 Reading; Unit 11 Vocabulary

Listening

Go over the IELTS tasks with the students and make sure they understand what they will practise in this section.

There are two listening passages. The first is a talk in by a careers advisor. The second is a lecture about employer selection tests.

1 **Match the words in C with the definitions.**

Go over the words with the students and explain that they are all about jobs and careers.

Have the students match the words with the definitions.

Answers

1 job-hunting   2 CV   3 occupation
4 vocation   5 recruitment   6 training

2 **Work in pairs. Decide which things the Careers Advice service does.**

Put the students in pairs and have them discuss what they think the Careers Advice service does.

At the end of the discussion, get the answers from one or two pairs and write them on the board. Explain to the students that they can check their ideas in the next activity.

Open answers

2.32 3 **Listen a conversation in the Careers Advice Service and label the plan.**

Direct the students to the plan.

Ask the students to listen to the conversation and label the plan. If you wish, you could ask the students to check their answer to activity 2 at the end of the first listening.

The Careers Advice Service has information on courses (prospectuses, booklets) and businesses, gives workshops on writing CVs and interviews, books places on careers fairs, has information on the latest jobs and has a computer program for career planning.

Answers

1 reading room   2 careers information room
3 computer cluster room   4 seminar room
5 career advisors' offices

2.32   Now listen again and complete the table with no more than three words.

Go over the table with the students and ask them to listen for detail and complete it.

Play the listening passage again and have the students complete the table.

Answers

1 an interview   2 organisations   3 vocational training   4 vacancy system   5 daily   6 career
7 interviews   8 prospects

4   Work in pairs. Answer the questions.

Go over the questions with the students and have them answer them.

If you wish, you could play the listening passage again for the students to check their answers.

Answers

1 the reading room
2 It asks questions and gives advice.
3 The first year, or as soon as the student knows what he or she wants to do. So that they can give advice about things to do alongside the course.

Now discuss which part of the Careers Advice Service you think is the most helpful.

Put the students in pairs and have them discuss which part of Careers Advice is the most helpful.

At the end of the discussion, get the answers from one or two pairs.

Open answers

5   Work in pairs. Ask each other the questions.

Go over the questions with the class and have the students discuss them.

At the end of the discussion, get the answers from one or two pairs.

Open answers

6   Complete the sentences with words and phrases in D.

Go over the words with the students and explain that they are all types of reasoning.

Have the students complete the sentences with the words and phrases.

Answers

1 abstract reasoning
2 diagrammatical reasoning
3 aptitude
4 verbal reasoning
5 numerical reasoning

Background reading

It is becoming increasingly common for employers to test graduates using psychometric tests. These tests were developed in the last century, but in the 1970s were adapted for recruitment purposes. The most often tested abilities are verbal reasoning and numerical reasoning. Below is an example of a verbal reasoning test question.

Many organisations employ students over the summer. Permanent staff often take their holidays over this period. Furthermore, companies often have a larger amount of work in the summer and need extra staff. Summer employment also attracts students who may return as well qualified recruits when they have completed their education. Making sure that the students learn as much as possible about the organisation encourages their interest in working on a permanent basis. Organisations pay students a fixed rate without holiday or sick leave.

Choose A, if you think the statement is true. Choose B, if the statement is not true. Choose C, if you cannot say.

1 It is possible that permanent staff who are on holiday have their work done by students.
   A B C

2 Students in summer employment are given the same pay as permanent staff.
   A B C

3 Students are subject to the organisation's rules.
   A B C

4 Some companies have more work to do in summer when students are available for vacation work.
   A B C

Listen to the Careers Advisor's talk and tick the correct column.

Go over the table with the students and ask them to listen for detail and complete it.

Play the listening passage and have the students tick the correct column.

Answers

	aptitude test	personality test
has a time limit	✓	
has multiple-choice questions	✓	
has no correct answer		✓
the person's score is compared with other people's scores	✓	
	✓	
has many parts	✓	
honesty is important		✓

8 Read the notes below and discuss the possible answers.

This activity aims to improve the way students approach such questions by using prediction to help them into the task.

Go over the notes with the students and ask them to discuss the possible answers.

Open answers

2.33 **Now listen again and complete the notes. Write no more than three words for each answer.**

Play the listening passage again and have the students complete the notes.

Answers

1 measure
2 the beginning of
3 number of statements
4 at working with
5 logical
6 more important
7 word
8 your reaction
9 your attitude
10 enjoy working

9 Work in pairs. Discuss the questions.

Go over the questions with the students.

Put the students in pairs and ask them to discuss the questions.

At the end of the discussion, get the answers from one or two pairs.

Open answers

➤ **Further practice:** *Achieve IELTS Workbook*, Unit 11 Listening

Writing

Go over the IELTS tasks with the students and make sure they understand what they will practise in this section.

1 Label pictures A–C with the words in E.

Direct the students to the pictures and ask them to label each one with words from E.

If you wish, you could ask the students which industries are shown, and if there are similar industries in their hometown or city.

Answers

A service industry (a call centre)
B traditional industry (basket weaving)
C heavy industry (steel making)

Now work in pairs. Discuss the differences between the kinds of industries.

Put the students in pairs and have them discuss the differences between the types of industries.

If you wish, you could write these ideas on the board to help the students: pay, work environment, health and safety, job satisfaction, stress, and so on.

Open answers

2 Read the title below and underline the key words.

Go over the title with the students and ask them to underline the key words.

Suggested answer

Since the eighteenth century <u>technological advances</u> have <u>replaced people</u> in the workplace. With today's technology this process is happening at a <u>greater rate</u>. <u>Technology</u> is increasingly <u>responsible</u> for <u>unemployment</u>. To what <u>extent</u> do you <u>agree</u> or <u>disagree</u> with this statement.

3 Read an answer to the title in 2 and complete the notes.

Refer the students to the passage and ask them to read it and complete the notes.

If you wish, at the end of the activity you could see which student gave the best excuse.

Open answers

4 **Read the e-mail below and answer the questions.**

Go over the questions with the students, then ask them to read the passage and answer the questions.

Answers

1 He missed his alarm call.
2 He was very embarrassed.
3 The tutor thinks Paul hasn't done any work.

Now read the passage again. Underline the phrases that show how Paul felt.

Ask the students to read the passage again and underline the phrases that show how Paul felt.

Answers

It's been one of my worst days of my life. (line 1)
My tutorial was absolutely awful. (line 1)
I was so embarrassed. (line 4)

5 **Decide which three words in A mean *a brief description*.**

Refer the students to A and ask them to decide which words mean *a brief description*.

If necessary, ask the students to read the reading passage in activity 4 again.

Answers

outline   summary   rundown

Not *presentation* or *project* as these can be a long pieces of work (see Unit 6).

2.37 6 **Listen to a conversation and circle three letters A–E.**

Go over the sentences with the students and ask them to listen for general understanding and circle three letters.

Play the listening passage and have the students choose three letters.

Answers

A   B   E

2.37 **Now listen again and complete the table. Write no more than three words for each space.**

Go over the table with the students and ask them to listen for detail and complete it.

Play the listening passage again and have the students complete the table.

Answers

1 tutorials   2 lectures   3 long essays

7 **Write a study timetable for yourself.**

Ask the students to write a study timetable for themselves. If any of the students are to take IELTS in the near future, you may wish to ask them to write a timetable towards this.

Now work in pairs. Compare your timetables.

Ask the students to work in pairs and compare their timetables.

Open answers

➤ **Further practice:** *Achieve IELTS Workbook,* Unit 12 Study skills

Listening

Go over the IELTS tasks with the students and make sure they understand what they will practise in this section.

There are two listening passages: a lecture about the memory and a workshop about good study habits.

1 **Do the quiz.**

Go over the quiz with the students and explain any unknown words, for example *keen* (very interested in something) and *jump right in* (start some immediately without thinking about it).

Tell the students they will discuss their answers in the next part of the activity.

Refer the students to the key for the answers and make sure they know the meaning of the new words as they will need *auditory* for activity 3 in the listening section.

Open answers

Now turn to assignment 12.1 and read your results. Work in pairs and discuss your answers.

Ask the students to turn to assignment 12.1 and check the results of the quiz.

Put the students in pairs and have them discuss their answers.

At the end of the discussion, get the answers from one or two pairs.

Open answers

2.38 2 **Listen to a lecture and write the appropriate letters A–C against the questions.**

Go over the notes with the students and ask them listen and complete them with A, B or C.

Play the listening passage and have the students complete the notes.

Answers

1 C 2 B 3 B 4 A 5 A

Now match the words in B with the definitions.

Go over the words with the students and explain that they are all from the listening passage and are all about memory.

Tell students that they will learn another meaning of register from the meaning used in Unit 1 (to put your name on a list).

Have the students match the words with the definitions.

Answers

1 retention 2 rehearsal 3 retrieval 4 register

2.38 3 Listen again and complete the notes. Write no more than three words for each space.

Go over the notes with the students and ask them to listen and complete each space with no more than three words or a number.

If you wish, you may want to ask the students to try to predict what kind of information, or which word, could be the answer.

Play the listening passage again and have the students complete the notes.

Answers

1 well-organised 2 registration 3 sensory memory 4 hold information temporarily
5 story 6 knowledge 7 auditory memory
8 visual

4 Work in pairs. Discuss which things can help you study.

Go over the activities with the class and have the students discuss them.

At the end of the discussion, get the answers from one or two pairs.

Tell the students that they will be able to check their answers in the next part of the activity.

Open answers

2.39 Now listen to a seminar and tick the things you hear.

Play the listening passage and have the students tick the things they hear.

Answers

being interested in the subject ✓
drinking water ✓   take short breaks from studying ✓   avoiding food with lots of sugar ✓
sleeping ✓   reviewing your work ✓   relaxing
✓   being positive ✓

Not mentioned: writing things down, listening to music

Additional activity: ordering information

If you wish, you could play the passage again and ask the students to number the things in the order they hear them. In this case, you could ask the students to do the next activity from memory.

Answers (in the order mentioned in the recording passage)

1 relaxing 2 drinking water 3 avoiding food with lots of sugar 4 short breaks from studying
5 sleeping 6 being interested in the subject 7 being positive 8 reviewing your work

2.39 5 Listen again and choose A–C.

Go over the multiple-choice questions with the students.

Play the listening passage again and have the students choose the correct answers.

Answers

1 B 2 A 3 B 4 A 5 B

6 Work in pairs. Ask each other the questions.

Go over the questions with the class and have the students discuss them.

At the end of the discussion, get the answers from one or two pairs.

➤ **Further practice:** *Achieve IELTS Workbook,*
Unit 12 Listening; Unit 12 Vocabulary

Open answers

Writing

Go over the IELTS tasks with the students and make sure they understand what they will practise in this section.

(Note: the text in activity 2 was written and adapted from an answer by a student from Hungary).

1 Work in pairs. Ask each other this question.

Go over the question with the class and have the students discuss it.

At the end of the discussion, get the answers from one or two pairs.

If there is an area common to all the students, you may want to give additional practise in this

Open answers

2 **Read the title below and underline the key words.**

Go over the title with the students and ask them to underline the key words.

Suggested answer

In some traditions <u>memorising information</u> given to students by a teacher is an <u>important method</u> of learning. Other educational traditions ask students to <u>find information by themselves</u> and place <u>little importance</u> on <u>remembering</u> it. The role of <u>memory</u> in <u>education</u> is <u>unimportant</u>. Do you <u>agree</u> with this?

Now read a student's answer and match the paragraphs with the summaries.

Ask the students to read the passage and match the paragraphs with the summaries.

Answers

1 B 'there is a big difference between the modern western-european way and the old fashioned eastern-European way' (lines 6–7)
2 D 'I think extremes are never good' (line 20)
3 C 'I remember my first language lesson' (line 15)
4 A 'we start memorising from the day we are born' (lines 1–2)

3 **Decide what the student's main point is. Circle A–C.**

Ask the students to decide what the writer's main point is.

Answer

B

Now work in pairs. Decide if you agree or disagree with the writer.

Put the students in pairs and ask them to discuss which points they agree or disagree with.

Open answers

4 **Read the passage again and ...**

Ask the students to read the passage again and find the mistakes.

Answers

1 *leon* (lion), *scools* (schools), *childrean* (children), *contryes* (countries), *hole* (whole), *dilog* (dialogue), *countyes* (countries), *extrimes* (extremes)
2 *western-european* should be 'western-European', *italian* should be 'Italian'
3 *many times* should be 'often', *once listened* should be 'immediately', *brains* should be 'mind'

Now correct the grammar mistakes.

Go over the grammar points to look out for with the students and ask them to read the passage again and correct the mistakes.
1 *on* should be 'in' (line 4), *with* should be 'in' (line 17)
2 *by memory* should be 'by memorising' (line 2), *in express* should be 'expressing' (line 10), *of travel* should be 'travelling' (line 14)
3 *let you to find* should be 'let you find' (line 18)

Achieve IELTS: assessing your essay

It is very important for the students to make time to re-read and check their essays when they have finished. Explain to the students that the 40 minutes suggested for this writing task includes not only planning time, but also time for checking and proofreading.

Go over with questions with the students – the questions will help each student to assess their essay in order to correct or revise it.

5 **Work in pairs. Read the title below and underline the key words.**

Go over the title with the students and ask them to underline the key words.

Suggested answers

Without intelligence it is impossible to be successful academically. <u>Intelligence</u> is the <u>most important factor in academic success</u>. Do you <u>agree</u> or <u>disagree</u> with the statement?

Now work in pairs. Discuss the title and make notes and an essay plan.

Ask the students to make notes for the essay title and structure these into an essay plan.

Remind them to use examples, and that these examples can be from their personal experience or from outside.

6 **Write the essay. You have 40 minutes.**

Tell the students that this is test practise and ask them to use their notes and plan from the previous activity to write the essay.

When they have finished ask them to go over the questions in the *Achieve IELTS* box and re-read their essay.

Now work in pairs.

Student A, give your essay to Student B and take their essay. Student B, give your essay to Student A and take their essay. Check each other's essay for spelling, punctuation, vocabulary and grammar.

Ask the students to swap essays and check each other's essay for mistakes.

Encourage the students to be helpful rather than critical.

Go round and monitor the students, helping where possible.

At the end of the checking period, put the students in pairs and ask them to go through the corrections with their partner.

See page 111 for suggested answer and commentary.

➤ **Further practice:** *Achieve IELTS Workbook,* Unit 12 Writing

Reading

Go over the IELTS tasks with the students and make sure they understand what they will practise in this section.

The reading passage is about a little explored, but potentially important physical condition.

1 **Match the words in C with the pictures.**

Have the students match the words with the pictures.

Answers

1 purple   2 turquoise   3 yellow   4 black
5 grey   6 burgundy

Additional activity: colours

Ask the students if there are any other colours they would like to know the words for.

Alternatively, you could point to the students clothing or belongings and ask them if they know the colour in English.

---

2 **Work in pairs. Answer the questions.**

Go over the questions with the class and have the students discuss them.

At the end of the discussion, get the answers from one or two pairs.

Open answers

3 **Read the title of the passage. Decide what the passage is about.**

Ask the students to work in pairs and decide what the passage is about.

If you wish, you could write their answers on the board for them to check back with later.

Now read the passage and choose the most suitable headings for sections A–D.

Go over the list of headings with the students.

If you wish, you could direct the students to the picture and ask them: 'What do you think it is? What does it do? How does it work? What is it called (*MRI* – magnetic resonance imaging)?'

Ask them to read the passage and choose the most suitable heading for sections A–D.

Answers

A i 'Now scientists from the University of Melbourne are researching synaesthesia' (lines 6–9)

B iii 'In most people, a physical stimulus presents a single sensation: light gives us a visual sensation, sound an auditory sensation, smell an olfactory sensation. Synaesthetes, however, get an extra one or more sensations.' (lines 21–26)

C vi (there are examples throughout the paragraph)

D vii 'The study found that ...' (lines 62–63)

4 **Do the statements agree with the information given in the reading Passage?**

Go over the statements with the students.

Ask them to read the passage again and decide which statements are true, false or not given.

Answers

1 True – 'their results have begun to reveal the secrets of how the brain functions' (lines 11–12)
2 False – 'They have colour as an extra bit of information to help them remember things' (lines 30–31)
3 Not given – the passage states that synaesthetes are 'creative, artistic and emotional', not forgetful
4 True – 'start happening from early childhood and they are highly consistent over time' (line 47–48)
5 True – 'appears to have a genetic component' (line 69)

5 Find words in the passage which mean ...

Ask the students to read the passage again and find the words from the context of the passage.

Answers

1 reveal   2 stimulus   3 sensation
4 consistent   5 component

6 Complete the table with words from the passage.

Ask the students to look quickly through the passage again and find words to complete the table.

1 visual   2 auditory   3 smell

Now read the passage again and complete the summary. Choose one or two words from the reading passage for each space.

Ask the students to read the passage again and complete the summary with one or two words from the reading passage.

Answers

1 brain images   2 perception   3 memory
4 the same   5 women

Language study: gerunds

7 Study the examples and explanation.

Go over the examples and explanations with the students.

Gerunds are a potentially difficult area of English and we have attempted to give a few simple rules. Explain to the students that these rules are simple guidance.

The basic uses of the gerund here are: as the subject of the sentence, after some prepositions, and after certain verbs including *stop, start, avoid, practise, finish, enjoy, suggest*. Using a gerund or infinitive after some verbs like *remember* and *forget* can slightly alter the meaning of the sentence.

Now complete the sentences using a gerund or an infinitive.

Go over the sentences with the students and ask them to complete them with a gerund or an infinitive.

Answers

1 seeing   2 having   3 to do   4 planning

➤ **Further practice:** *Achieve IELTS Workbook*, Unit 12 Language study

Pronunciation

2.40 **8 Listen and practise, paying attention to the /ŋ/ sound.**

If you wish, you could play the recording and have the students write the words as well as practicing saying them.

➤ **Further practice:** *Achieve IELTS Workbook*, Unit 12 Pronunciation

9 Work in groups. Discuss the questions.

Go over the questions with the class and have the students discuss them.

At the end of the discussion, get the answers from one or two pairs.

Open answers

➤ **Further practice:** *Achieve IELTS Workbook*, Unit 12 Reading

Speaking

Go over the IELTS tasks with the students and make sure they understand what they will practise in this section.

1 Answer the questions for yourself.

Go over the questionnaire with the students and have them answer the questions and complete the first column.

Open answers

Now listen to three people and complete the table.

Ask the students to listen to three people and complete the table for them.

> **Additional activity: note taking**
>
> If you wish, you may like to play the passage again and make notes on what the speakers say.
>
> Ask the students to write the reasons the speakers give and what they say in more detail.
>
> Ask the students which speaker they are like, if any of the three.

Answers

	Speaker 1	Speaker 2	Speaker 3
1 Do you have a good memory?	Quite good	Yes	No
2 Have you got a good memory for …			
A names?	Sometimes	Yes	Some
B faces?	Yes	Yes	No
C dates?	No	Yes	Usually remember some dates
3 What was the last thing you forgot?	Sister's birthday	Five things on a shopping list	House keys

Express yourself: rephrasing

Listen and practice the expressions.

Go over the expressions with the students.

Remind them that they will be able to use these in the speaking test.

Play the expressions and have the students listen and practise them.

If you wish, you may want to play the recording before the students practise the expressions, and ask the students to mark the stressed words and intonation.

Now work in pairs. Ask each other the questions in 1 and complete the table for your partner.

Put the students into pairs and have them ask each other the questions and complete the table.

Try to encourage the students to use the phrases for rephrasing.

Open answers

2 Match the sayings with the meanings.

Go over sayings 1–5 and explain they are all about remembering and forgetting.

Explain that sayings 1 and 2 may be useful during the speaking test if they cannot remember a specific word.

Have the students match the words with the meanings.

Answers

1 c 2 d 3 b 4 e 5 a

Now work in pairs. Discuss any similar sayings in your language.

Ask the students if there are any sayings associated with remembering and forgetting in their language, or if they have the equivalent of 1–5.

3 Read the candidate task card below. Decide what the overall topic is about.

Answer

Studying and education

Work in pairs. Student A, you are the examiner; interview Student B. Student B, you are the candidate; answer the questions.

Put the students in pairs and go over parts 1 and 2, the rounding-off questions and part 3 with them.

If you wish, you could refer Student A to assignment 9.2 for the examiner's script.

4 **Now change roles. Student B, you are the examiner; interview Student A. Student A, you are the candidate; answer the questions.**

Have the students change roles and repeat the speaking test.

Suggested answer

I agree with the first part of the statement, but not with the second. It would not be possible for an unintelligent person to achieve academic success, however intelligence may not be the most important attribute of a good university student.

First of all, I consider motivation to be a crucial factor. A student who is attending university merely to satisfy his or her parents' ambitions is less likely to succeed than one who has a genuine interest in the subject. For example, a student who attends a course in order to gain the qualifications to take over the family business will probably not have the same level of incentive to study as a psychology student who is genuinely fascinated by the workings of the human mind. The latter will be motivated to make more of an effort outside the classroom in independent research.

Secondly, I would maintain that good study skills are equally valuable. An intelligent student who is lazy or badly organised is more likely to fail a degree course than a student of average ability who always completes assignments on time, attends all lectures and seminars, and has good study habits. Modern degree courses demand that students are able to work without supervision for three hours or more per hour of tuition. The ability to memorise information and pass examinations no longer guarantees a good grade.

In conclusion, although intelligence is definitely an asset, other factors such as interest in the subject and self-discipline are equally, if not more, relevant to academic achievement. In my opinion, training in study skills should form part of the preparation for any degree course, and students should take time to carefully consider their choice of subject before they enrol.

Student's answer

Nowadays intelligence is very important in all aspect of live. I want to start my argument with an Afghan saying. It says, 'An inteligent enemy is better than a stupid friend'.

In today's world, everything around us is work of inteligent people. For example, the development of the computer made life very easy, simple and more convenint. If we compare life in the past and in the present. Today one computer can do the jobs of ten people. In addition, intelligence has made possible space travel and the discovery of universal secrets. If there is no intellegent people, this would have been impossible. Furthermore, man is facing chalange of global warming. According to a new scienic report, the Artic has decreased in size over the last thirty years. Warnings to avoid fussil burning and benzine emission, has been made by intelegent people who provide this information for the people in order to protect them and the planet.

To conclude, all of these are impossible without intelegence. I think all developments which we see around the world is work of intelegent people.

> ### Comment
> This essay is under length and does not address the task. The writer has made no reference to academic achievement. Lexical errors are frequent and may cause problems for the reader. These factors would probably limit the score to a band 5.0.

Achieve IELTS: end of course review

1 **Which area of the test do you think you have improved at most?**

Reading ☐
Listening ☐
Speaking ☐
Writing ☐

2 **Which other areas have helped you most?**

Language study ☐
Expressions ☐
Exam help (*Achieve IELTS* boxes) ☐
Pronunciation ☐
Study skills (*Achieve IELTS Workbook*) ☐

3 **Which unit did you find most interesting/remember best?**

_____

_____

4 **Which area would you like to review/practise more?**

Reading ☐
Listening ☐
Speaking ☐
Writing ☐
Language study ☐
Expressions ☐
Exam help (*Achieve IELTS* boxes) ☐
Pronunciation ☐
Study skills (*Achieve IELTS Workbook*) ☐

5 **Other comments**

_____
_____
_____
_____
_____
_____
_____
_____
_____
_____
_____
_____
_____
_____